Ellen Putnam Day

Some Chronicles of the Day Family

Ellen Putnam Day

Some Chronicles of the Day Family

ISBN/EAN: 9783743349902

Manufactured in Europe, USA, Canada, Australia, Japa

Cover: Foto ©ninafisch / pixelio.de

Manufactured and distributed by brebook publishing software (www.brebook.com)

Ellen Putnam Day

Some Chronicles of the Day Family

CHRONICLES

1750–1850

LAKE WARAMAUG

SOME CHRONICLES OF THE DAY FAMILY

COMPILED BY

E. D. P.

CAMBRIDGE
Printed at the Riverside Press
MDCCXCIII

To the Memory of

HARRIET DAY ANDREWS

WHOSE CHARACTER

OF RARE PURITY AND SWEETNESS

ENDEARED HER TO EACH MEMBER OF OUR FAMILY

THESE ITS PAST CHRONICLES

ARE DEDICATED

PREFACE.

THESE Chronicles were compiled at the request of my cousins, — the great-grandchildren of the Reverend Jeremiah Day, of New Preston.

I have sought to preserve the continuity of family life rather than to make biographical studies.

If the " Day Sisters," as we call them, can thus be brought before the minds of our descendants with even a small portion of the interesting character and charming personality that we have known in full, a large part of the purpose of these Chronicles will have been accomplished.

E. D. P.

December, 1892.

PART I.

THE PARSONAGE.

"Honor thy father and thy mother, that thy days may be long in the land which the Lord thy God giveth thee."

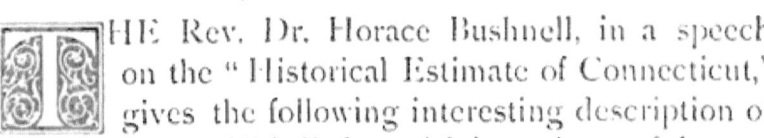HE Rev. Dr. Horace Bushnell, in a speech on the "Historical Estimate of Connecticut," gives the following interesting description of New Preston: "This little parish is made up of the corners of three towns, and the ragged ends and corners of twice as many mountains and many-sided hills. But this rough, wild region bears a race of healthy-minded, healthy-bodied, industrious, and religious people. They love to educate their sons, and God gives them their reward. Out of this little obscure nook among the mountains have come forth two presidents of colleges, the two that a few years ago presided at the same time over the two institutions, Yale and Washington or Trinity. Besides these it has furnished a secretary of state for the Commonwealth during a quarter of a century or more; also a member of Congress; also a distinguished professor. And besides these, a greater number of lawyers, physicians, preachers, and teachers, both male and female, than I am now able to enumerate. Probably some of you have never so much as heard the name of this little by-place on the map of Connecticut. Generally it is not on the maps at all, but how many cities are there

of 20,000 inhabitants in our country that have exerted one half the influence on mankind? The power of this little parish, it is not too much to say, is felt in every part of our great nation. Recognized, of course, it is not; but still it is felt." It is unnecessary for us to add that the greatest prophet who arose in this live little parish was the man who wrote these words and classed himself humbly among the "other preachers and teachers too numerous to mention."

It was in this parish of New Preston, and during the years when these very persons were growing to manhood, that our great-grandfather served as lifelong pastor. We have little to say of his ancestors. We know of Robert Day, who came to this country in 1634, and in 1636 followed Hooker across the wilderness, shaking the dust of the future "Hub of the Universe" off his feet, to settle in Hartford; but we know little of his descendants, except their orderly existence in the genealogical records, until we come to Jeremiah Day, who was born in Colchester, Conn., in 1737. His father, Thomas,[1] was a farmer, and moved from Colchester to Sharon in 1755. As far as we know, all the Days before him, back to the original Robert, were men and women of plain, simple lives, but perhaps with some leaning towards letters. Certainly our great-grandfather, Jeremiah, showed such a tendency so strongly that his father decided to send him to college, and he entered Yale, and was

---

[1] The three male ancestors between Robert and Jeremiah were all named Thomas. This is interesting to us, as our grandfather was given the family name, and it has descended to son, grandson, and great-grandson.

graduated in 1756. He studied theology with Rev. Joseph Bellamy, D. D., of Bethlehem, Conn., and later with Rev. Cotton Mather Smith, of Sharon, and was ordained[1] in 1770 at New Preston. He was married three times. His first wife was Sarah Mills, of Kent, who had one son, Mills, who lived less than a year. His second wife was Lucy Wood, of Danbury, who had no children, and lived but a short time after their marriage. Then in October, 1772, he married Abigail, widow of Sylvanus Osborn, and daughter of Stephen Noble, of New Milford. She had four sons and one daughter. Abigail Noble was born in 1740. She too came of plain farming people. Her father, Stephen Noble, lived most of his life in Kent, where his son and grandson lived after him. He was a man of very simple habits; he was an early riser, and for many years before his death was said to take nothing but "rusk and milk for his supper."

It is hard for us to picture the farmers, or more properly freemen, of a hundred and fifty years ago. They were certainly not like those we are familiar with now, and although their lives were in one sense plain and homely, yet they were far from being illiterate. There was a great deal of high thinking with their plain living, and we fully believe that an ancestry of that type is of a kind for which to be grateful. The conditions of their lives certainly did not foster ambition, nor cultivate those qualities of mind which mark men of striking talent or imagination, but we believe that to such ancestors one owes those sterling virtues which must be the background of all noble

[1] Appendix.

character, and which carry one through life's hard places with a steady face to the front. The will of Jonathan Day, the brother of our great-grandfather, of which he was made executor, gives us a glimpse of those homely days. After disposing of his real estate and making several small bequests in money, it goes on : —

Item. — To my loving sister, Sarah Downs, I give one of the cows that I have let out to Deacon Jackson, to be delivered to her in the spring of the year 1765. *Item.* — To my sister Tamar's three children, namely, Jonathan, Tamar, and Sarah, I give to each of them a cow, and my will is that when Jonathan shall arrive to the age of twelve years, my executor shall let out the cow that is for him, and that she, and her increase that may be for him, shall be let out for his interest until he shall arrive at the age of twenty-one years. And also that when my sister's two daughters, Tamar and Sarah, shall severally arrive at the age of ten years, that the cow for each of them respectively, shall be let out in the manner aforesaid, and delivered to each of them when they shall arrive at the age of eighteen years, or at the day of marriage, if either of them should marry before they come to that age.

We wish we had any way of obtaining a picture of our great-grandfather's early life and training, for his letters prove him to have been a man of rather uncommon character. All his letters show that, while not theologically in advance of his time, he was yet distinctly open-minded. He has been described as a "man of sound understanding; not a fervent but an impressive orator in the pulpit, and a man whose advice was much sought in all ecclesiastical difficulties." We have ample testimony to the latter in the letters we find addressed to him from different pastors. In December, 1774, one Asahel Heart, who was pastor of a church in North Canaan, writes: —

REVEREND SIR, — There are difficulties subsisting here in this church, which for a considerable time have hindered us from enjoying the ordinance of the Lord's Supper, which greatly threatens the peace, union, and prosperity of our little flock. Whereupon, by the mutual agreement of those concerned, you, sir, are hereby desired as one of the members of council, to meet the others Tuesday evening the 2d day of February next, — by your endeavors to remove our present grievances and lay a hopeful foundation for a future permanent gospel union and peace among us.

This is only one of many such appeals.

Then there are letters from young students asking advice and counsel. Innumerable controversies, also, were carried on by letter with ministers in all parts of the country. These have no part in this little sketch, but we quote from two letters as samples of his style in writing. One is evidently the rough draft of a letter sent to a brother minister, but it bears no address. The subject might almost be called the Relations of Church and State: —

March 30, 1779.

REV. AND DEAR SIR, — This acknowledges the receipt of your letter of March 10. It turned in my mind that perhaps we had continued the dispute as long as would be profitable. I was therefore pretty much resolved to desist. But upon a little further thought I concluded it might be proper to minute down some few cursory reflections not cast into argumentative form. I profess to be entirely upon the side of liberty in the matters of religion; nor do I conceive I have advanced anything inconsistent therewith; neither am I for blending civil and ecclesiastical matters together.

I think, as I have stated the matter, the civil magistrate confines himself to his civil province when he makes provision for the gospel ministers. Nor is this making ministers tools or engines of state, because in their religious character they are under the control of no human laws whatever. I cannot but think there are advantages (mercenary views aside) in ministers having state salaries and a legal right to recover them. How much is a competent support, can be agreed upon between the minister and the people. The minister in this way knows what to depend upon, and whereas, if matters are left at utter uncertainties, when and where and what, and how much, the people shall give him, he may be perplexed to know how to order his temporal affairs. You say he may trust Christ. But I am ignorant of any promise of Christ that he will provide for us if we neglect proper means to provide for ourselves. Neither ministers nor people ought to be influenced with a view to filthy lucre. Yet where is that Scripture which forbids ministers to provide and lay up for themselves and families any more than it does the people. I am not sensible there is greater temptation to avarice and worldliness upon my plan than upon yours, provided you maintain that your ministers should be supported, though it were at the expense of excommunicating every member of your church. And I think it saves a minister from being under the temptation to condescend to the humors, caprices, and corruptions of his congregation, for fear, if he should displease them, they should withdraw their favors, on which he is dependent for daily bread. After all, if it was inconsistent with any of the rights of Christians or any law of Jesus Christ, I would instantly renounce it, but I am not convinced that it is. If the religion of Jesus has been the occasion of disturbing the peace of society, it is not because there is any proper tendency thereto, but because of the corruptions of man counteracting the genuine tendency of religion which requires its votaries to live peaceably with all men. As to that objection against my plan, that it favors heretics equally with the orthodox, I say, let the heretics enjoy this privilege. The way to destroy heretics is not by depriving them of the common privileges of mankind, but by the force of reason and truth.

We believe this letter to give a very true view of our great-grandfather's character, conservative in methods, yet liberal in mind, as shown in his remarks about "heretics;" upright, and with a sturdy self-respect and strong sense of justice, as may be seen in his independence, and in his scorn of that curious mental condition which seems to make it possible for many good ministers to think that because they are ministers, God will assume their neglected duties and responsibilities. The only other letter of this kind we will quote is one written to Dr. Jonathan Edwards, 2d. The two seem to have corresponded for some years, but there are not many letters preserved. The one from which some extracts are given is evidently one of several which passed between them on the subject of "Infant Baptism." It is closely written and very long, and would hardly edify us if given entire.

NEW PRESTON, *November* 16, 1790.

REV. AND DEAR SIR, — I thank you for your kind favor; both for your books and your remarks. I agree with you in thinking that there has long been need that the subject of "Infant Baptism" should be searched to the bottom. I believe the Baptists increase in this country (they certainly do about us). This was the reason of my preaching and printing upon the subject. Books of that kind are very rare in these parts. From this consideration I was prevailed upon to publish what I thought might contain a summary of the arguments on the subject. I had regard to a small circle and not to general utility. A thorough, particular, and critical discussion should be assigned to more able hands than mine. It would be very grateful to me, if you would undertake this business. I should, however, be glad to see what has been written pro and con, and if you could favor me with the loan of those books you mentioned, it would be an additional kindness. I read Lothrop's first edition several years ago. I have hardly had time as yet to thoroughly peruse the pamphlets you sent me, so as to form a competent judgment concerning them. Dr. Gill, however, appears to write with great dogmatical assurance and a degree of petulancy. I question whether his naked arguments are possessed of invincible force. Foster pretends to great honesty, and I will not dispute the sincerity, but I must take further time to judge of his merits as a disputant. Some of his reasoning, however, is obviously little better than mere chicanery. But to go on to the remarks. I am glad you have made them; more of the kind would still oblige. But suffer me to say a few words in my own defense.

Here we are plunged into an argument concerning the identity of the Jewish and Christian churches and the rites of circumcision and baptism, after which he proceeds: —

Infants were taken into the Jewish church, and if the Christian church be the same, infants also have a right to be taken into that; the Jewish church had an external mark of being the people of God, which was circumcision; the Christian church has an external mark of the same thing, which is baptism. Many are the advantages which would flow from an initiatory rite, which would be a common advantage to each church. Jewish parents were, in consequence of circumcising their children, obliged to teach them the divine law, instruct them in their religion, and, by all the motives which it suggests, persuade them to the practice of it. If these and such like reasons are in favor of infant circumcision, are they not equally, nay more so, in favor of infant baptism.

We read nothing in these letters of "Infant Damnation." The question seems to be purely one of infant *versus* adult baptism, which arose (as he says) "through the increase of the Baptist denomination bringing the subject to notice."

These two letters seem to give a fair sample of his mind and character as shown in what might be called his professional correspondence, and we need not dwell longer on this side of his life.

But how they did love to talk and argue in those days! The correspondence begun with Jonathan Edwards in 1790 seems still in progress in 1795, and we know not how much longer. They lend each other books and then discuss them on closely written foolscap. But they always close with " Yours with profound esteem and brotherly love."

As early as 1797, New Preston was sufficiently public spirited and enterprising to have started already a public library, for in that year Thomas Day, in New Haven, received a letter from his father asking him to purchase " all John Newton's works, Baxter's 'Saints' Rest,' and Swift's 'Laws of Connecticut,' " adding, " Let Mr. Beers know they are for our public library, and I know he will make a discount." [1]

The family life seems to have been a very happy and united one. If his advice was sought by those outside his circle, it is certain, also, that his sons were in the habit of referring everything to this simple country clergyman, whose acquaintance with the

---

[1] Since writing the above we have found a letter from the historian, Benjamin Trumbull, to our great-grandfather, making inquiries about New Preston. From notes jotted down on this letter we learn that the public library was instituted in 1792.

world at large seems to have been confined very nearly to his four years in Yale. We have no clew to the early life, for no journal has been found, and it is not until the boys leave the home and go out into the world, and letters begin to pass back and forth, that we can find any suggestive threads out of which to weave a tale.

The oldest son was sent to college, but the second, Thomas (our grandfather) was intended to stay in New Preston and take charge of the farm, which must have been of some extent, and a great burden to his father. In after years our grandfather used to show his children an old stone on the hillside, upon which he sat down one hot summer day, in the midst of the haying season, his whole soul in revolt, and from which he arose with the firm resolve that he would never be a farmer. Here we see one of the first instances of that gentle wisdom which always seems to have guided the father in his dealing with his children. The country pastor remembered his own early struggles, and with a strict sense of justice forbore to urge his son to the farm life which had failed to satisfy his own aspirations. So he saw each one of the sons leave the home and go forth to make a larger career for himself. And it is not hard for us to picture with what intense gratitude and thankfulness he rejoiced over their worldly success (which he lived long enough to see in some measure assured) and the noble and upright characters which that wider field helped to develop and mature.

The parsonage was beautifully situated on a hilltop, near Lake Waramaug. This lake is one of the loveliest in New England, with wooded hills all about it, and "Pinnacle Mountain" rising to the height of one thousand feet at its eastern end. It is between three and four miles long, and yet barely half a mile wide, so that, as it curves among the hills, it seems more like a river than a lake. In the time of which we are writing, the lake seems to have been so identified with the people who lived about it, that in the letters we find its name abbreviated, and constantly used when speaking of their New Preston friends, as "What do you hear of the 'Ramaugers?" "Some of the 'Ramaugers were in New Haven to-day." One of the grandchildren, writing in after years of her first home after she was married, says: "You can hardly imagine how very quiet it is, unless you let your mind go back to New Preston, and those summer afternoons when we sat on the front steps and saw only the ripening grain waving in the sunlight, and that was all that moved." It is difficult to realize how inaccessible was this little village in those days. We judge by the letters that a good part of the journey was necessarily made on horseback, and a family with one horse was often greatly perplexed as to its method of transportation, — as when the father writes: "I have been thinking how to get you home after examination. Jere has taken the horse to Williamstown. I shall have to hire one if I send on purpose for you." Often the two brothers made their trip home from New Haven over the hills to New Preston, on the same horse, "riding and tying," sometimes in bitter cold weather, and sometimes under burning suns. What a primitive, honest community it must have been! One brother rides ahead a few miles, then ties the horse by the roadside and trudges on, sure that no one will touch or harm it, until the other brother overtakes it, mounts and rides again ahead to leave the horse in his turn. What a welcome they had at the parsonage! And did not dear mother Abigail have a rousing good supper for them, and pet her boys to her heart's content?

The few letters we have of Mrs. Abigail Day's give us the impression that with a loving, earnest nature, she combined a mind of much less serious cast than her husband's, and was possessed of a sense of fun and humor which we think must have brightened the old home a good deal. Three anecdotes are extant in connection with her, and they are each very suggestive. She was very fond of horses, and apparently fearless in the saddle, riding much about the country on a horse kept for her own use. Once when her horse was disabled she asked one of her neighbors to lend his horse to her for the afternoon. He thought it too spirited a horse for a lady to ride, and at first refused, but finally agreed to let her have it if she would not take a whip, as the animal "would not stand it." When she returned the horse and was asked whether she had been able to manage it, her reply was, " I found him pretty slow at first, but I rode up under an apple-tree and cut off a good long switch, and then he went famously." The following story was told the writer, on her only visit to New Preston, some years ago. In primitive days they had their evening meetings at the hour of "early candle-light." Every one came to church bearing his own candle, which was lighted just before entering the church door. It is said, that in a spirit of mischief our great-grandmother Abigail stood just within the door, in the darkness, and dexterously blew out each candle which the worthy parishioners held out before them, to see their way over the threshold. This, for the minister's lady, was certainly a naughty trick, and we fear it occasioned much talk in the parish, to have been remembered over a hundred years. But what a picture is brought before us! How we should like to look in upon one of those services! The plain, bare country church; the rugged, labor-worn faces of the farmers and their tired wives (for who ever heard of a farmer's wife who was not tired) bending over their psalm-books; all the light in the church coming from the candles or tallow-dips. What shadows were there! and how many Rembrandts are lost for lack of an interpreter!

Another story, of her courage and presence of mind when a girl, is told by one of her grandchildren:[1] "A hundred and fifty years or more ago, when Grandmother Day was a girl, living in New Milford, Litchfield County, she went with some of her young friends to gather the wild strawberries which then, as now, grew freely on the hillsides and meadows in that region. The country was only partially settled, and rattlesnakes haunted their old homes among the rocks. The girls in frolic tried to alarm each other by cries of 'rattlesnake' from different parts of the meadow, but for a time none were seen. Later, Abigail strayed into another field at some distance from her companions, where she found the berries large and ripe.

[1] Mrs. Holly.

While busily picking she suddenly saw a snake glide past her, and, with the ominous rattle, disappear into a hole among the rocks. She called out 'Snake, snake!' but they had been too often alarmed for no cause to take any notice of it now, and she was left to abandon the field or fight for possession. So arming herself with a strong stick she proceeded to attack the enemy. The prodding of her stick brought him out of his hole, and as he came head first, she easily dispatched him. Then thinking there might be young ones in the nest, she ran her stick in again, and killing each one as it came out, she remained mistress of the field. Fearing that on account of their many jokes about the snakes, her story might not be credited, she carried her dead victims in her apron back to her home." There are no pictures in existence of either the minister or his wife, but one who remembered them told one of their grandchildren that the minister was tall and fair, and his wife, short and slightly formed, with dark eyes and hair.

In those days, as we know, the pastors sometimes went off on missionary tours through the less settled parts of the country. In 1788 our great-grandfather went on such a one in the State of Vermont. With his journal kept during that tour we find a letter from his wife. This is addressed to "The Rev. Jeremiah Day, itinerating in the state of Vermont." The modern post may be more rapid, but can it do more than carry a letter to the person addressed? and faith and friends seem to have carried this one to its destination.

September 19, 1788.

MY DEAR, — This morning I received your letter, dated September 9, by Mr. Hillhouse. It is like cold water to a thirsty soul. I am anxious for your safety and happiness. Fear and surmise put on a thousand forms of dear disquietude, and round my ears whisper ten thousand dangers. Our family has, through the Divine Goodness, enjoyed as good a state of health as usual since you left us. May God preserve us all from every evil, and grant that you may do much good in a short time and return to us in safety, that we may rejoice together in His goodness. Mr. Farrand and Mr. Bordwell have taken their turns in preaching here. Mr. Bordwell sends compliments, and wishes you may be the means of making the " wilderness blossom as a rose." Our business within doors and without goes on as well as can be expected in your absence.

September 20. Mr. Gold has just come to take his turn here. Mr. Worden has lost his youngest child the week past. It is past ten o'clock, and I must conclude,

Subscribing, your ever dutiful

ABIGAIL DAY.

Is there not a delightful touch of wifely human nature in the desire that he will do "much good in a short time"?

In his journal we read: —

September 1. Set out on my tour to preach in the State of Vermont. Went through Litchfield, dined at Captain Osborn's. Arrived at Mr. Mill's about sun an hour high. The roads very much gullied by the late rains and the riding bad.

September 3. Rode from Mr. Badger's to Mr. Collins's, in Lanesborough, thirty miles. From the upper end of Blandford Street, the mountains northward present a curious, romantic appearance, many of them in the forms of pyramids, and almost contiguous.

September 4. Set out from Mr. Collins's about nine o'clock, and arrived at Mr. Swift's, at Williamstown, about one o'clock, fourteen miles. By the way my mare went lame, lost off one shoe ; got her shod : cost 1/3. At Williamstown the mountains around are exceedingly lofty and majestic.

September 6. Called on Dr. Shephard. Made a visit at Mr. Branch's. Ruminated on what to preach the next day.

First Sabbath, September 7. Preached A. M. from Isaiah i. 18 ; P. M. from Luke xiv. 22.

September 8. Rode about twenty-five miles.

Second Sabbath, September 14. After meeting went about two miles to see a sick man. He appeared to be much concerned about his soul, and was very free to talk upon things of another world. I tarried there all night.

September 15. Rode to Colonel Stone's at Bridgeport. Preached there in the afternoon.

September 17. Went forward to Panton ; dined at Henry Spalding's ; preached in the afternoon in his barn. After preaching, proceeded, with the intention to arrive at New Haven Falls, but was prevented by missing my way, and was obliged to lodge at a Dutchman's hut. Through an assault of fleas and agitation of mind slept none all night.

September 29. Went to Burlington ; dined at Judge Lane's ; with him went to Colonel Sexton's, where we held meeting. After meeting walked down with Colonel Sexton to the bay, from where was a beautiful view over the lake, which is here about sixteen miles wide.

October 5. Preached at Mr. Foote's, at Middlebury. Baptized two children, one named Electa, daughter of George Sloan.

October 7. Came to Rutland ; tarried at Mr. Hibbard's. The road now begins to be good.

October 13. Wanting some linen washed, I stayed here [Middletown] to-day. It snowed most of the afternoon. I preached in the evening at Joseph Rockwell's. Tarried at Mr. Rockwell's all night.

October 24. Took leave of Mr. Sill, whose kindness and friendship to me have been singular.

October 26. Preached at Pownall. The greater part of the people are Baptists. Two Baptist preachers were present when I preached. I have now completed my mission in the

State of Vermont. The people have in general given good attention, though the assemblies have been commonly small.

October 27. Horse shod, 1/6. Proceeded homewards.

October 29. Arrived at my own home. Found my family fairly well. Have had an agreeable tour, upon the whole. Have abundant reason to recognize the providential goodness of God. Blessed be His name forever!

There is a journal of another tour made to the Susquehanna in 1794, but the incidents are too similar to make it worth quoting. He visits two sick children and prays with them, baptizes other children; marries some few persons, and even buries some. The last entry is: —

November 1, 1794. Arrived home about seven o'clock, considerably wet with the rain; in good health, however, and found my family so. Traveled six hundred and ten miles, gone sixty-two days, and preached fifty-one times. *Laus Deo!*

Every letter from the father and mother among the hills carries earnest wishes for the spiritual welfare of their boys. In 1797 the father writes to Thomas:

You have almost finished your academical education, and will soon be called to improve your talents and acquirements in some way, wherein you may be useful to mankind and yourself. Be not transported with the deceitful pomp of this world: "The fashion of this world passeth away." Be, above all things, concerned to secure to yourself a happy immortality in a future world. You will soon have accomplished the short career of this life, though you should live to old age. You owe yourself and your all to God, and ought to be devoted to his service.

And again, in another letter about the same time:

Some business you must engage in for support in this life; but it is of still greater importance we should be prepared for a future, and that you improve all your acquirements and talents to the glory of God and in usefulness to mankind. . . . Money, whatever it may be called, is not the *main thing;* the truly one thing needful is something different and infinitely more important, — it is a heart devoted to the service of God.

Thomas, it is evident from all the letters, was the cause of much anxious thought to his parents during his college course. The oldest son, Jeremiah, had inherited the simple, unquestioning faith of his parents, and had naturally a religious turn of mind. Thomas's mind, on the other hand, as is shown by the very choice of his profession (that of the law), was given to subtle thought, and could not easily run in the groove marked out for it. His temperament, also, was susceptible to the fascinations of the world, or, as his father puts it in one of his letters to him, "If you know your own self, you must be sensible that you have a variety of biases which will be ruinous to your eternal welfare." With this constant solicitude for him, and regarding him as probably in much greater danger than it is possible for us now to believe him to have been, his parents dealt with him with tenderness and wisdom which we cannot too much admire. Never a word of command, no prohibitions, and all admonitions given in tender love; and if the phrases seem a little stilted to us in these latter days, we may be sure they did not sound so to the son who had been brought up in the simple home of the old clergyman. He is just about to leave college, and writes to his father for advice about taking charge of a school in New York. His father replies, April, 1797: —

With regard to the advice which you wish me to give you relative to your taking a private school in New York, I have hardly had time or means of knowledge to determine on its expediency. That you should engage in some employment which may afford you the means of subsistence will doubtless be necessary; teaching school most readily offers itself. But as to the most eligible place I am in doubt. Two or three things ought to come into view to give the decision, — lucrativeness, security of morals, and advantages for improvement in useful knowledge. How the proposed place will conduce to any of these I cannot tell. There are doubtless good characters in New York, and many more whose examples might have a corrupting influence unless very vigilantly guarded against. It will probably be expensive living there. What wages they will give, you do not know, nor what advantages you will be under for scientific acquirements. On the whole I am inclined to think a place in the country might be found preferable to New York, where you might be nearer your friends, less exposed to temptation, and be in the way of fitting for some future occupation. Whether it would be best to go to New York for getting better information about the school, — I should have no objection to it were it not for the cost, which would be considerable for one who has so little to spare unnecessarily. You are soon to look out for yourself in order to get a living. I can't help you to much more money. You have need to use the greatest prudence and economy, or you will soon find yourself in distressing circumstances, which will be the more distressing as you have not been used to the greatest frugality. Some attention ought to be paid to your temporal welfare, but I am much more concerned for your future interest. Time is nothing to eternity, and it is but of little consequence how we fare in this world, provided we may secure the everlasting inheritance. I send you herewith $40, also a little budget containing a shirt, etc. We have heard from Jere; I believe about three weeks ago ; that he was then well. Noble lives with Colonel Tallmadge, at Litchfield. The agricultural business devolves on Mills, and it appears to be rather discouraging to him that he is left alone, and has to do all the drudgery, while his other brothers are living (as he thinks) in scenes of pleasure. If you take a tour to New York you need not get a piece of linen, as you proposed, because we have sent by Mr. Leavitt for a piece, and soon expect it.

From your affectionate father,

JEREMIAH DAY.

This letter is surely a very wise one. The matter is put clearly before his son, but there is no urging of his own views or assuming responsibility. We have no doubt it seemed to the father that it would be, from all human points of view, absolute ruin for his boy to go to New York, but he was content, after simply telling him what he thought about it, to leave it in God's hands; and we cannot doubt that at morning and evening as the daily prayers were offered up in that little country parsonage, so far away from all the allurements of the world which seemed threatening to draw their beloved boy, there was always added the petition that God would guide his choice aright. We know at least that he did not go to New York, but instead to Williams College, where he succeeded his elder brother in the office of tutor.

Thomas studied law with Judge Reeves, in Litchfield, and in the fall of 1799 was in Hartford preparing to be admitted to the bar. That he was in some pecuniary difficulty, is shown by a letter from his father, dated October, 1799: —

You don't know what to do. Alas! I am little able to tell you. The way to guard against evil is to look out beforehand and make calculations with such judgment as in an ordinary course of nature will succeed, and never to depend on capricious chance. The laws of nature are inflexible, and without the means the desired end is not to be expected. Cannot you get the chance of instructing some youth, or some such occasional employment which may contribute to your help for the present. It must be very expensive living at Hartford, and whether it is the most eligible place in your situation, I am not certain. I shall wish to know whether you are admitted to the oath at the next court or not, and what your prospects are with respect to getting into business, etc. From your affectionate father,

J. DAY.

The oldest son, Jeremiah, taught school directly after leaving college, and soon supported himself, but Noble needed money as slender capital upon which to start in his business life, and Thomas a longer training to fit him for the profession of the law, which he had set his heart upon following. The demands for money were incessant, and it is pathetic to read of the efforts made by the father to supply them, for this was always done, though at the expense of much toil and close economy in the remote country home. Later, when Thomas is settled in Hartford and waiting for clients to come, the father, in reply to another request for money, sends a letter which is worth quoting.

NEW PRESTON, *April*, 1800.

Money! money! money! The very cry which lately resounded from France. I do not wonder America was alarmed. The cry has force enough to rouse apathy itself. Within three days I have received three letters from as many of my boys, in each of which money is fervently solicited. Is New Preston a mint, or is it another Potosi, that it should pour forth such copious streams of money as are asked for? In this case must there not be want of economy and a well-directed application to business? "Cut your coat according to your cloth," is an old and significant adage. If we are poor we must retrench our expenses and avoid every superfluity. We should keep an account of all our expenditures, and be sure not to have them exceed our income. A little progress in ascending a hill is encouraging, and gives hope of reaching the summit, but if, while we get forward one step we fall back two, it portends no good. Pride and vanity cost a poor man twice as much to support them as they are worth, while humility and prudence more than doubly pay for their inconvenience. Were I able to supply all your present wants, it would on the whole be no real advantage to you, but a calamity; but the truth is I am not able to afford you such supplies as you want, and at the same time do justice to my other children (or indeed furnish them with what they really stand in need of). I know not how to accomplish this spring's exigencies. Noble wants $500. Mills must be maintained at college, and you must know how costly that is from your own experience. I see no way, therefore, but that you make the best shift for yourself that you can.

From your affectionate father,
J. Day.

And, again, about the same time he writes: —

Let me know what your prospects are and what advantages you are under for improvement. Perhaps you may get into some little pieces of business which do not directly come into the line of your profession, which may afford you a little help for the present; such little jobs are worth looking at by one under your circumstances. You must be vigilant and prudent, and intent on your occupation if you would expect to obtain a handsome living by it, or be eminent in it. But whatever anxiety you may have for this life, I wish you to have a still greater for the world to come. What is time to eternity, the body to the soul, or the greatest affluence on earth to the heavenly inheritance? Therefore seek first the kingdom of God, and all other things necessary shall be added.

In the "Connecticut Evangelical Magazine," which we shall have occasion again to quote later, we read the following: "The salary stipulated by the society at the time of his settlement was seventy pounds annually, to be paid one third in cash, and two thirds in wheat at four shillings per bushel, and iron at twenty-four shillings per hundred. Notwithstanding this stipulation, he in fact received a considerable part of every year's salary in mechanics' work and labor on his farm at the ordinary price, without any deduction.

"In the revolutionary war he suffered with his brethren. In addition to the usual ministerial indulgences at that period, he remitted in the year 1776 five pounds of the nominal amount of his salary. This sum was remitted in the first instance for that year only, but was continued in each succeeding year, not only during the American war, but till his death. His proposals exhibited to his parishioners were in the following words: 'Considering the greatness of the necessary expenses of the country at the present day, and the difficulty of the times, and being willing to contribute my proportion towards the public expenses, and to encourage the glorious cause in which we are engaged, I am induced to give five pounds lawful money the present year to this society, to be deducted out of my salary for the year 1776, which is more than two shillings on the pound of all my ratable estate, and I furthermore make declaration and promise that all those who are bound by law to pay rates to me, but profess to be of any other religious denomination from us, if they will produce good and creditable certificates that they have paid for the support of the gospel to the amount of their rates to me for preaching which they have enjoyed within the compass of this year, that is to say, from the first day of February, 1776, to the first day of February, 1777, shall, in consequence of application made to me for the above mentioned year, receive a full discharge of their ministerial taxes. That they should be required to pay something for the support of the gospel is reasonable, inasmuch as a preached gospel is a benefit to civil society as well as to the souls of men.'

"This voluntary relinquishment of salary to relieve his parishioners, and promise to pay to the society the legal taxes of all dissenters, operated as a direct tax of ten per cent. annually on all his ratable property for thirty years. It ought, however, to be remarked, in justice to the society, that in the year preceding his death, they made him a present of about the same amount which he had annually relinquished to them for their peace and prosperity."

On this appallingly small salary and the proceeds of his farm, our great-grandfather supported his sons through college, and settled them in life.

The year 1800 seems to be the beginning of a new era in the family life. All the sons now had left home. Jere was a tutor in Yale College; Thomas, admitted to the bar of Connecticut and waiting for clients in his office in Hartford. Noble was also in Hartford, "looking about," and Mills, the youngest, was in his freshman year at Yale, and looking forward to studying for the ministry. A different tone now creeps into all the letters. The sons have put away "childish things," and the two elder brothers discuss divinity, law, and politics, while the father no longer advises, admonishes, and instructs, but in his turn appeals for help and advice.

NEW PRESTON, *July* 24, 1800.

Come, I suppose you are poring over your mazy tomes on law, waiting in vain for some full-pursed client to invite you into active service. To arouse you a little from your dull slumbers, I will put a question to you. It is considerably interesting. I don't know but I shall have to go to law myself. You know there was a fine crop of wheat growing on the land which I sold to Scranton. I am told, though not from him, that he intends to keep the whole of it himself. This was far from any expectation of mine, and different from all the conversation we have ever had on the subject. But it is suggested to me that he means to try his title. Now the case is this. I had leased the land to him, though only verbally; he to return me one half of the produce. Before the time was out for which he took the land, he bought it, though this was considerably after the crop of grain was got in. He has a deed in common form. No written reservation has been made, and I am not certain I can make proof of a verbal agreement that I expressly reserved my half of the grain. It is likely to me that it will turn on the point whether, when a man conveys a piece of land with the grain then growing on it, he be entitled to the crop.

I wish you would consider this question, and form an opinion on it. And not merely on the question as here stated, but upon all the circumstances attending the affair, with which, I suppose, you are competently acquainted. And I wish you would advise with your more experienced brethren, and let me know, as soon as may be convenient, your thoughts on the case. Perhaps I have trusted too much to his honesty, and have not taken care to have everything explicitly expressed in writing, which might have been more prudent. But I supposed our understanding of matters was perfectly alike, and that there would not be the least disagreement.

Your affectionate father,
J. Day.

It is amusing to find the father making use of his son's legal knowledge thus early, when during previous years he seems to have had a partially expressed regret, that a son of his should choose so worldly a profession. Jeremiah too, wrote many a long letter to Thomas, upholding the study of divinity against that of the law. In one of these letters, after dwelling upon the different evils necessary to contend with in the study of the law, he says:

> As to the study of divinity in contrast with this, no comparisons are necessary from me. It contains the spirit of all law, both human and divine, stripped of technical shackles.

We may agree heartily with this sentiment, and yet we do not find that it prevented the author of it from placing all his business affairs in his lawyer brother's hands, and looking to him constantly for advice.

Indeed, it is apparent that Thomas, who, with his more flexible temperament and inquiring mind, was a source of anxiety to his father and elder brother during his college life, early acquired a steadiness of purpose, a clear judgment, and an unselfish and upright character, which made him a comfort and help to them both, as long as they lived. We have only one letter from Thomas to either of his parents, and since it was written to his mother in 1801 we give it here.

HARTFORD, *July* 25, 1801.

Dear Mama, — I shall improve with pleasure every opportunity to inform an anxious parent of my welfare. My health is evidently better than it was in the spring, and my eyes have not only recovered from their inflammation, but are considerably stronger. I have had the use of the Averills' horse a part of the time, and have had Jere's horse here two or three weeks. About a fortnight ago I rode him down to New Haven and left him there to be put out to grass, on account of a bad cough he had caught by keeping him upon hay. Since that time I have rode less, but have continued other means of exercise which have generally answered the purpose very well. When I was at New Haven, Jere was so ill that he did not attend college exercises. His disorder appeared to be in his lungs, and occasioned his spitting blood. He appeared, however, to be cheerful and in good spirits. Whenever his friends asked him how he did, he told them they must ask the doctor, for he did not know himself, but that he was well enough. I saw the president [Dr. Dwight] in Hartford, one day this week, and he told me that Jere was better, though he had not yet returned to the instruction of his class. While looking around for some little tribute of filial affection, I observed, the other day, in one of our stores, a silk shawl which I thought would be very proper for a woman of your age and situation in life. I send it with this letter, and hope you will be pleased with it, not only on account of its intrinsic worth, but for the motive from which it was procured. I intended to have sent the new saddle which I purchased some time ago, by a team, yesterday; but accidentally I missed of the opportunity. I am told, however, that there will be more teams in, next week, by some of which I will endeavor to send it.

THOS. DAY.

It is a matter of regret that this silk shawl is not in existence. We should like to see what was considered suitable for her "age and situation in life."

The eldest son, Jeremiah, entered Yale in 1789, but his health broke down, and he was obliged to leave before his course was finished; he recovered, however, and returning to college, was graduated with "high honors" in 1795. He then went to Greenfield to take charge of the school left vacant by the appointment of Dr. Dwight to the presidency of Yale. After a year there, he went to Williamstown, where he was tutor until, in 1798, he was elected tutor at Yale. In 1801 he was elected to the professorship of mathematics and natural philosophy, but his health again failed, and in the fall of that year he went to Bermuda. This was a most anxious time for the father and mother. The change did not seem to benefit him greatly, and in April he returned to New Preston. At this time Thomas and Noble were in Hartford, and Mills at college, so that he was alone at home with his parents, and, we judge by the letters, in a very depressed state of mind and body. The mother writes to Thomas:—

December 19, 1802.

MY DEAR SON,—I have not complied with your request to write every week, but I do not forget you. I expect you have heard by Mr. Abernethy, and your father wrote you the particulars you wished to know; he is now gone to New Milford to give them a Sabbath's preaching at their request. He is not as well as when you were at home, but continues to preach. Jere is much as when you were here, only he has not had so much fever, nor so much distress of mind; but he thinks he has reason to be as much concerned as ever, and is greatly alarmed at times that he should be so stupid about the everlasting welfare of his precious soul. I think, whenever his anxiety of mind increases, it increases his fever, and he thinks it is hectic, but the doctor says he thinks it is not. The weather has been so cold he has not rode any for a week or two past, but sometimes walks as far as the store. Oh, Thomas, see that you prepare for death while in a state of health. A time of sickness is a poor time to have that great work to do. My love to Noble. Tell him I fear he takes too much care for the things of this world to give himself time to prepare for eternity. " For what shall it profit a man to gain the whole world and lose his own soul."

From your affectionate mama,   A. Day.

Our little sketch does not aspire to be a family biography, and so we will give here in rapid outline only the main facts of our great-uncle Jeremiah's life.

The doctor seems to have been right; Jere recovered his health, and returning to college, entered upon his work as professor of mathematics and natural philosophy. He continued in this until he was chosen successor to Dr. Dwight as president of Yale College in 1817. He held that position until 1846, when he resigned on account of ill health and (as he may have thought) the infirmities of age, being then seventy-three years old. He lived twenty-one years longer, and died in 1867, at the age of ninety-four, greatly beloved and esteemed.

After this time almost no letters are preserved from the parsonage. The letters which pass between the two brothers, Jeremiah and Thomas, contain constant reference to the old home, and mention of their visits to their parents, and often they agree to meet in New Preston on their vacation trips, but there is little to suggest much more of the home life. In a letter to Thomas, Jere says : " Noble was at home last week. You will probably wish to learn how our parents are. To use the elegant language of Colonel Manby, 'They are in health, and transmit you their blessing by me. The venerable pair totter on the verge of a well-spent life, and only wait to see their children settled in the world to depart in peace.'"

In 1800 the "Connecticut Evangelical Magazine" was started, and the Rev. Jeremiah Day was invited to be one of the board of editors. He seems to have had some doubts about accepting. He writes to Thomas: "I have not *absolutely* refused to accept the appointment to be one of the board of editors, though I wished to be excused. I find the infirmities of age growing upon me, and family cares are about as much as I can attend to, without involving myself in public concerns which are not unavoidably connected with my profession."

His objections seem to have been overcome, however, for we find his name on the title-page of the first volume as one of the editors. We have no idea what his contributions were to this periodical. He seems to have been fond of making verses. A great number of his poems are preserved, but truth compels us to admit that whatever gifts our great-grandfather possessed, he had not those of a poet. His verses rhyme, but they do not ring. There are a number of rather long poems. One, on the "Pleasures of a Country Life," in Goldsmithian style, we have dutifully perused, and we feel sure that it can be spared from these Chronicles. There are others on "Independence," "Elegy on the Death of General Washington," "Address to a Stupid Mortal," "Worth of Time," "Intricacy of Providence," and many more with funeral hymns and epitaphs, apparently composed on the death of some of his parishioners.

He died in 1806, and his wife survived him four years. This division of our story is fitly closed with a portion of a sketch of him, written by the Rev. Azel Backus, and published in the "Connecticut Evangelical Magazine," shortly after his death.[1]

"In private life, in the domestic relation, Mr. Day afforded as perfect an example as human nature has produced since families were formed. To his wife he was all that her fondest wishes could claim or ask. To his children he was the best of fathers. The exclamation of one of his sons on the mournful occasion of his death, to a friend, was as just as it was pathetic: 'How kind, how tender, how indulgent, and yet how faithful our father has been, four hearts will remember, and while they remember, will swell with gratitude and affection, till every emotion shall be extinct.' In all his intercourse with his people he was grave, serious, and instructive. Wise as a serpent and harmless as a dove, he was one of the most illustrious examples of ministerial prudence. As a divine he had sound understanding, capable of deep research in the science of theology. Though not a fervent and animated orator, he was a solemn and impressive preacher. With a clear, luminous method, he loved chiefly to dwell on the great doctrines of divine grace and the distinguishing truths of the gospel. To his brethren in the ministry he was a tried friend and an

---

[1] Dr. Azel Backus was the first president of Hamilton College, New York; born in Norwich, Conn., 1765, was graduated at Yale in 1757, and succeeded the celebrated Dr. Bellamy as pastor of the church in Bethlehem, Conn. He was considered somewhat of a wit.

able counselor, — in ecclesiastical councils and difficulties his advice much sought and improved. Indeed, in this important branch of ministerial duty, he may not have left a parallel. Always upright in his views, remarkable for punctuality in attendance on all appointments, and able to seize the right point in every question, able to disentangle the most embarrassed subject, clear and conclusive in his reasonings, fellow-members in council always felt themselves honored when they found his opinion to coincide with theirs.

"Always humble and exemplary and abounding in the work of the Lord, he appeared to be filled with love for the souls of men and to have a special regard to the spiritual interest of his own particular people. For many years he labored with them to little apparent effect, but not long before his death God granted a very considerable revival. His brethren in the ministry are witnesses of his strong emotions when reciting to them the evidences that the pleasure of the Lord was apparently prospering in his hands. At the meeting of the association of which Mr. Day was a member, in May last, the good man attended, as he said, and as it proved, for the last time. His youngest son was examined and licensed as a preacher of the gospel. Although he said little, his tears and expressive countenance when his son retired, showed that the feelings of the aged Simeon were throbbing at his heart. He frequently remarked that death had no terrors for him, and that if it was the will of God, he did not wish to live *beyond his usefulness.* At a time when three of his children were with him, a few weeks before his death, he told them with perfect composure and serenity that he had but a little longer to stay with them. The disorder of which he died was supposed by his physicians to be dropsy in the breast. This occasioned considerable difficulty in breathing, and consequent distress. But he can hardly be said to have complained at all. His sufferings were known only from involuntary expressions of his countenance, from his struggles, and from his mild and simple answers to the questions put to him.

"Mrs. Day, however, who watched every breath he drew and felt every pang that he felt in his sickness, thinks that his sufferings were at times extreme. His strength was not so much impaired but that he walked across the room and sat in his chair a considerable part of the time, on the very day of his death. He prayed in his family every morning and evening during the whole of his sickness, not excepting the last morning of his life. Did he survive his usefulness?

"He died about nine o'clock, Friday morning, September 12, in the seventieth year of his age."

THANKSGIVING HYMN.

Henceforth the mercies of the Lord
Shall be a sweet constraining cord,
To bind my soul in willing chains
To praise Him with melodious strains.

Now I resolve thro' grace divine,
The Lord shall be forever mine;
Urged by the impulse of His grace,
I'll run with speed the heavenly race.

His goodness shall fresh life impart
Athwart the passions of my heart,
And all my pow'rs with pleasure draw,
In prompt obedience to His law.

JEREMIAH DAY.

PART II.

"Religion delights both in reminiscence and in anticipation. . . . The identity of God's eternal being stretches under and gives consistence to our fragmentary lives. God's eternity makes our time coherent." — PHILLIPS BROOKS.

JEREMIAH and Abigail (Noble) Day had four sons. Of Jeremiah, the eldest, a slight sketch has been given in the first part of these Chronicles. Noble entered upon the precarious career of a business man, and after living some years in Hartford, returned to the old home in New Preston. The latter part of his life he spent in the home of his son, Henry Noble Day, who was then professor in Western Reserve College, Hudson, Ohio. He died there, in 1855. He had six sons and two daughters. The sons and one daughter lived to grow up, but their lives do not belong to our sketch.

Mills died when twenty-eight years old, while tutor at Yale. From the very few of his letters which we have been able to see, we judge him to have been a gentle, serious-minded fellow.

Thomas, the second son, our grandfather, after studying law in Litchfield, settled in Hartford, and in 1813 married Sarah Coit, of Preston, a town about five miles from Norwich, Conn. She was the daughter of Wheeler and Sibyl (Tracy) Coit. Wheeler Coit was a descendant of John Coit, who came from Wales about 1630.

The grandson of John, the Rev. Joseph Coit, was born in New London, was graduated from Harvard in 1697, and took the degree of M. A., on examination, at Yale in 1702. He married Experience Wheeler.

Their son Samuel married Sarah Lathrop, and Wheeler Coit was their fifth child. He was born in Preston in 1739. He was a merchant, and appears to have been a "man of influence and high standing in the community." He represented Preston in the General Assembly of 1793, and died, in 1796, of yellow fever, which he contracted in New York.

Mr. Wheeler Coit was a widower with two children when, in 1774, he married Sibyl Tracy.[1] The eldest of these children, Lucy, was married twice: first to Edward Ledyard, Jr., and afterwards to Thomas Fanning. Thomas Fanning must have been a friend of Mrs. Coit's before her marriage, as may be seen by an interesting letter written to Mrs. Sibyl Coit, in 1776, when his future wife, her stepdaughter, was only ten years old. The letter is worth giving as a whole, though it has no especial connection with our annals.

CAMP AT ROXBURY, March 22, 1776.

DEAR LADY, MRS. SIBEL COIT, — I have now before me your much esteemed favor of the 17th inst., by Mr. Wright, and only want words to express the honor done me thereby. Think not, my worthy friend, that a disregard has prevented my writing to you long since. The great hurry of public business which I have passed through has prevented my writing to many of my friends (though never out of mind),

---
[1] Appendix.

among whom, permit me to assure you, I esteem you one of the nearest ; and though a happy change of state has placed you in a different station than when I wrote you formerly, yet I trust it has not lessened your esteem of those who were then happy in your friendship and acquaintance. Sure I am, could I have a thought different from this, my happiness would be much diminished.

I have, on your recommendation, with that of your sister, endeavored to show Mr. Wright the respect of complaisance that I was master of, though small. I think, from the slight acquaintance I have yesterday formed with him, that he is much of a gentleman. I have procured a pass for him to go into the town, but could not be permitted to accompany him. Before this reaches you, the great news of our taking possession of the town of Boston will be with you. At ten o'clock, Sunday last, the troops evacuated the town in the greatest hurry and confusion, and I believe were faithfully frightened by our near approach to them on Dorchester. At twelve o'clock, such of the army as had had the small pox, to the number of fifteen hundred, from this camp and Cambridge, marched into and took possession of the town. In this party I had the pleasure to enter the town, and of being witness to the highest scene of joy that ever fell to my lot to be a spectator of. The excess of joy of those of your sex could not be hushed ; wringing of hands and crying for joy was only to be heard through the whole street, with "Welcome ! welcome, our dear countrymen ! We are glad with all our hearts to see you." Their sincerity could not be doubted. I find the town not so much damaged as I expected. The most has fallen on the poorer people, as the houses were mostly old that were destroyed. Those more elegant were improved by the officers of the army and navy, and are left in good order, except being very dirty.

The tories and unfriendly part of the inhabitants are mostly gone, with their families, and have robbed the town of almost all the valuable effects. The churches are mostly damaged; in particular, the noted Old South, which was improved for a riding-school, having all the pews and pulpit taken away, the floor taken up, and an elegant plain with dirt laid in its place. Will not the Most High revenge Himself for such profanation of His synagogues and temples?

The fleet are yet lying below the town, which makes us think they have thought of paying us another visit; but we wish for nothing more, as our army would gladly meet them.

Miss Polly Cutter and Miss Sally Green, with whom you may have been formerly acquainted, are in town, but I think they are not very handsome. Mr. David Hubbard is also in town, and, I believe, would be proud to revive his former acquaintances, though he has had but little notice taken of him yet.

I must beg leave to refer you to the bearer, Mr. Wright, for many particulars which I am not able to write. Though [I] fully believe I wrote sufficient to tire your patience, and though much matter that seems more proper to write to my own than your sex, [I] trust you will pardon the digression on this extraordinary occasion. Please to make my compliments agreeable to your good gentleman, on his return from New York. Likewise, to Mr. D. Mason, and the ladies of your family. I have taken the liberty to inclose a letter for your sister. If she is now with you, please deliver with your own hand; if she has returned to Norwich, please to forward by safe conveyance. I will only add my sincerest wishes for as complete happiness to attend you and your family as I could wish for myself, and am your sincere friend,

THOMAS FANNING.

Sibyl Tracy Coit must have been an interesting woman. We have none of her letters, but occasional references to her, in her children's letters, give us many a hint of her character. Her eldest daughter, also named Sibyl (afterwards Mrs. Hezekiah Lord), was said to have much of her mother's "steady, equal mind." Mrs. Coit seems to have been a loving and warmly loved stepmother, if we may judge by a letter written by her husband's daughter, Lucy, who later became Mrs. Thomas Fanning.

DEAR MAMA, — Sibel wrote me your cough was a little abated, which I hope continues. Oh, dear, I can think of you, dream of you, but seldom can I see you. . . . An anxious imagination will sometimes present prospects which [neither] reason nor philosophy can restrain, for those we hold dear, who are at a distance from us.

This wise and tender mother, as she appears to have been, died in 1793, leaving six children, the youngest a boy only three years old. The two youngest girls, Sarah and Lydia, were always very closely united, and as their homes, after they were married, were for some years near together, we get through their letters written to the other sisters a fair picture of their early life.

The earliest letter which we have was written by Lydia when she was a girl of fifteen to her sister Sibyl, who was on a visit to New York.

LYDIA COIT TO SIBYL COIT.

PRESTON. *April.* 1803.

Letters were never more welcome than those from our dear sisters, which we received sometime since. We were very much entertained with the descriptions of the evenings you spent at church and the theatre. Think the one at church must have been very solemn and good, but as I never saw anything of the theatrical kind, can form no idea of that. I cannot but feel very glad that Mrs. Fanning is going to New York; it will seem quite like seeing you when she returns, and I know you will be quite happy at seeing her there.

Sally and I are going over to carry our letters and see Mrs. Fanning, as she goes early to-morrow morning. . . . Mr. Morgan is below, playing and singing "Hartford." He takes his final leave of us this morning to go to Norwich and teach a singing school. As I told you in my last letter that he was about to make a speech, I will just tell you that on Thursday (the singing-lecture day) he left his seat, went down, and " mounted the rostrum with a skip." If it was not time poorly spent, and what I think would be uninteresting, I would just give you the heads of his discourse. It began, " Respected singers." It was principally composed of extracts from Davies and Miss Moore. That part of it addressed to the treble began, " Virtuous and good as you are," etc. The girls are going to write, and therefore my letter is long enough.

With sincere affection, your sister,

LYDIA COIT.

This Aunt Lydia, according to all that can be learned of her, was a most lovely and lovable person. It is to her letters, which have been more carefully preserved than those of the other sisters, that we are indebted for an account of the family life during the first quarter of this century.

The oldest sister, Sibyl, was nine years older than Lydia, and after her marriage to Mr. Hezekiah Lord,[1] the two girls, Sarah and Lydia, found in him a most affectionate and thoughtful brother and adviser, as the following letters testify: —

HEZEKIAH LORD TO SARAH COIT.

NEW YORK, *September*, 1808.

MY DEAR SISTER, — Mrs. Lord had a letter yesterday from Mrs. Coit, dated at Stafford Springs, which gave her an alarming account of the health of our dear sister Hetty. If

[1] A merchant in Savannah.

it should be practicable, I should advise by all means that she should come to this city. The climate will be more favorable to her constitution, she can have as good medical advice as can be had in America, and all the comforts and luxuries that her situation may require. If it is agreeable to her to come, she will be a most welcome guest. Such an arrival would add to my happiness, and you know not how much your sister would be gratified to have her here. And you, Sally, will be received with equal satisfaction, for you are equally dear to us. My house shall always be a home for *you all* whenever it is agreeable to you to make use of it, in sickness or health. . . . Dr. Mason has returned to the city, and on Sunday he preached twice. His sermons were solemn and impressive; I cannot but esteem it one of the most valuable privileges to hear him.

Believe me, dear Sally, your affectionate brother,

HEZEKIAH LORD.

In 1812 he went abroad for some months, leaving the two sisters as companions to his wife, then living at No. 53 Sugar Loaf Street, New York.

II. LORD TO MISS SARAH AND MISS LYDIA COIT.

LIVERPOOL, *January*, 1812.

MY DEAR SISTERS, — Your letters and the "Orbit" were received the 1st inst., each of which afforded me especial satisfaction. If you have ever realized that I only expressed the feelings of my heart when I said I was happy to count you as a part of our family, you can readily imagine that that heart is feelingly alive to all your affectionate remembrance. I have always felt a deeper interest in your welfare than I have ever been able to express. . . . There are many little incidents in your letters interesting to me. That you have all been so well and happy, I esteem as a mark of great favor, and you can hardly realize with how much interest I hear that Mrs. Lord's health is better than usual. You observe that she will only give you some extracts from my letters, and that you had thought of applying for a permit to peruse them. But the Old Lady says, "No, that is left at my option." It sounds very like her, but she says truly. You know I repose especial confidence in her discretion. I know she *won't* expose me. Now say, whether I should do rightly, to the least degree, to abridge the trust that I have left with her. Besides, you will recollect that you do not like Mr. Newton's "Letters to a Wife," and how can you expect to derive either profit or pleasure from perusing mine? You perhaps will expect me to relate some of the novelties of this old world that must meet the eye of every common observer who abides in it only a few months, and I should be happy to gratify you, but my limits will not permit. I hope to treasure up something, and if ever we shall meet again by our own fireside, you shall have my narrative as often as it affords you any satisfaction. I now begin to look towards my native land with the hope of returning; it is the only prospect I can dwell on with any satisfaction, and I do not forget how much uncertainty there is in this. I have to cross the mighty deep, and although I may be mercifully preserved, there are of necessity many unpleasant things to encounter. But I will leave all to Him who knows what is best, and I hope always to feel due submission to every dispensation of a wise and holy Providence. I shall make the most of my time by addressing this letter to you both, and shall only add that I am as ever,

Your affectionate brother,
HEZEKIAH LORD.

In March, 1813, Sarah Coit was married to Mr. Thomas Day, and went to live in Hartford.

LYDIA COIT TO SARAH COIT DAY.
MIDDLETOWN, *June*, 1813.

I owe you much, dear Sarah, for your kind attention to my wishes. The detail was uncommonly interesting, and I rejoiced to hear from yourself that you were happy. If you praise that amiable new sister much more, I shall think you cannot love me any longer after the old sort, the disparity will appear so obvious. The news, or rather the confirmation that you received of news we had received, I was sorry to hear. I would rather be an almshouse dependant than a mischief-maker. After I parted with you I could not but feel a degree of solitude in the midst of my kind friends. Uncle Tracy returned in the afternoon, and was sorry he did not see you and Mr. Day. Miss Brigham seems a fine girl, very sedate and industrious, as is each member of this large family. Really, when we sit at table, it seems to me like Rockaway or Stafford — fourteen, with Miss B. and myself, is the regular number. Here the puzzle is, not to get little, but enough, and the point is daily effected through the medium of a very large pudding (of which all are glad to partake) and a loin of veal, or something equivalent, which would last the trio at your table a week.

One afternoon the sympathetic people of Middletown were employed in lamenting over New London, and the frigate destroyed by our *furious* enemy, the British. Mr. Vandusen set out at sunset for New London, like good old Priam, to claim his valiant Hector from the vindictive foe, but, behold! no harm was done; the fort and its captain, as well as the frigates, were safe. This afternoon we shall go out, I believe, to make a few calls; and if a private opportunity offers for my letter on Monday morning, I will send, for I shall be sorry not to write at all, or to have you pay eight-pence for what will not be worth one farthing. My pen does not act as though it had any split. You will remember my impressive requests, and tell Mr. Day if he will see it, he must receive it as Professor Hale requested he would his.

Sunday evening. I have written enough already, yet as talking to you yesterday does not suffice for to-day, I have left the little social party below for the purpose. Owing to Mr. Huntington's indisposition, there has been no preaching in his church to-day, so we wandered. This afternoon we stayed at home, and I thought more of my friends than my book. I am a little anxious to hear from them, scattered hither and thither as they are. I must close, as the bell rings, and my letter is going on a cruise to find an opportunity to sail for New Haven. Yours,

LYDIA.

FROM THOMAS DAY TO MRS. DAY.

NEW HAVEN, *October*, 1813.

MY DEAR SARAH, — My official duties press so heavily upon me that I have only time to write to say I cannot write. I arrived here in good season Wednesday. Under cover of a surtout and cloak, I could hardly fail of being comfortably warm; but I feared that you must have suffered considerably by the raw air in the afternoon. Last evening, my brother returned with his family. They are all in fine health; have hardly got settled yet. I shall expect a letter from you soon. Tell me all the particulars about everything that concerns you. Give my love to Hetty, Lydia, and everybody else that you love. I shall write more when I have time, but I shall be much occupied during the session.

As ever, yours, T. D.

LYDIA COIT TO MRS. THOMAS DAY.

NEW YORK, *April* 12, 1814.

MY DEAR SALLY, — Samuel announced to you my safe arrival, or I should have written before this the particulars of my journey. We had a pleasant ride to New Haven, where we were set down at four o'clock, and I concluded to go and see Mrs. Kingsley. She was going to have the two Mrs. Dwights to tea, but urged my staying and taking the stage from there, but Mrs. Silliman, who was going to have Mrs. Day and Mrs. Knight, very soon came over to wait on me there to tea, and though I should have liked to stay with

Lydia alone, [I] thought the change of parties would be agreeable, and accompanied her home. Mrs. Knight and myself were mutually pleased to meet. Mr. and Mrs. Day came very late, and I came away with my escort Joseph, Charles L., and Jonathan, very early, so that I did not see them as much as I should have been pleased to. They very politely invited me to go there, or to stop on my return; so did Mrs. Silliman, from whom I could hardly disengage myself. I believe we should love her as much as we do Mrs. W[adsworth]. We left New Haven at six o'clock, Friday morning, and after a day marked by nothing unpleasant (unless the deep ruts might be so esteemed) we arrived in safety precisely at ten o'clock in Courtland street; we soon proceeded down Greenwich Street. The stage had no sooner stopped than the door was opened by Mr. Coit, and I found my kind friends were awaiting my arrival, and at once gave me a refreshing cup of tea. A more affectionate welcome I could not possibly desire than I received from each one, down to little Harriet. Saturday I had a number of calls, went out shopping, ordered a chip hat with green wreath, and saw the extremes of fashion and folly.

Mrs. Brinkerhoff invited us to spend Monday with her. I dined there, but was engaged to Mrs. Perit for tea. Mrs. B. had a very handsome dinner. Her good minister, Mr. Matthews, made two calls while I was there, and that I thought the best of the whole, though Mr. B. opened his wine, but one shilling short of five dollars a bottle.

Tuesday morning [I] sallied out with Mrs. Coit and purchased sundries which you will receive by Jonathan. I cannot find a shawl to suit me, so I don't know but I must blindfold taste, put pride down, and wear my old one. Mrs. Smith is in worldly affliction; speculation has ruined her husband, but she is very cheerful. The old lady was to take tea at Dr. Mason's, and will send me word if he preaches in the morning. Miss Murray, a young Dorcas, is here cutting charity clothes; all interrupts me. New York is the same

as ever, continually something going on. My kind love to
your neighbors. I wholly forgot to offer to take commissions for them. Do offer for me.

      Yours and Mr. Day's affectionate
                Lydia.

LYDIA COIT TO MRS. THOMAS DAY.

         New York. *June.* 1814.

Dear Sally, — Yours of June 9th received last week, and I have been making the inquiries you desired about carpeting. The price is the monstrous one of fifteen shillings, so I presume you will rather keep pride at the bottom of the stairs than gratify him by purchasing at this time. Have you got a letter from me which went by a Mrs. somebody last week? I have now written our friend Mrs. W., and desire you to say to Mrs. Trumbull that I do not find exactly such a shawl as she wishes, but exactly such a shawl as her mother's; if she has anything new to add, she must write soon, as I suppose I must not purchase. . . . Old Mrs. Bowman and Mrs. Rodgers desired me when I wrote to remember them to you. The request has been repeated, and if it is not too laughable I must desire you to remember them back. Every one thinks I look strange without you, and I feel stranger. President Davis came in town. I was much pleased with him; he spoke of Mr. Day, and Mr. Perit mentioned my acquaintance with the gentleman. It would not be good for the vanity of either of you if I were to relate what he said. And I will tell you what gave me equal pleasure. On hearing who I was, he immediately said he well remembered my parents, or rather my father, and as so many seasons have passed since the place that once knew him was destined to know him no more, I was much gratified. Love to Mrs. Ely; the girls desire theirs to Mr. Day and yourself.   Your affectionate sister,

                Lydia.

LYDIA COIT TO HEZEKIAH LORD.

NORWICH, *February* 25, 1815.

MY DEAR BROTHER, — To tell you how glad the receipt of your letter, with that of our dear sister, made us would not be possible; we read them again and again, and I hope our joy was not quite unmixed with gratitude. I rejoice to congratulate you both on the return of peace, when the noise of war shall no longer be heard in our streets, be felt in our dwellings, nor desolate our borders. Various have been the expressions of joy, but nothing has savored of gratitude to Him, who has restrained wrath and returned in mercy. But the world will, I suppose, to the end of time, wear its own features. On Washington's birthnight, the English officers came in, attended a splendid ball, and partook of an elegant supper prepared at New London. The treaty has reached you, I suppose, and I can hear you both say, "What have we gained?" Every point conceded for which the contest was begun, and yet the administration call it a peace "highly honorable to this country." But stop; I do not want to write politics. I had rather tell you, if you have not heard it, that old Mrs. Johnson has at length got home. It was two or three months since, but I did not hear it until the other day. Mrs. Joshua Huntington was buried yesterday, and H. Williams, who is at their house, is not expected to live many days. Sibyl knows them well, and I mention this for her. I presume you seldom get a letter which does not mention the exit of some one from this scene of change, anxiety, and pain. Sometimes I think the period of your exile, as you term it, is done with the war, and I want very much to hear again from you.

Your affectionate sister. LYDIA.

LYDIA COIT TO MRS. THOMAS S. WILLIAMS.

... I want to send you congratulations on the return of peace. Sweet sound! but, as you say, there are joys departed which cannot be restored, and a treasury emptied which it will take years of prosperity to replenish. I had last week a letter from a cousin in New York, who told me she went to hear my beloved Dr. Mason preach, the Sabbath after the ratification of the treaty had been received. She said after service, he addressed his congregation on the news of peace, adding, that on the day the corporation should appoint for public rejoicing, he hoped to have the pleasure of seeing their faces in that place to unite with him in praising God for His wonderful kindness to us; for never, since the savior of his country was inaugurated first President, had we such cause for joy. The following Thursday, she dined at Mr. Bethune's, and, with a large party, went to the Orphan Asylum, where a nice dinner of roast beef and pies (in milk pans) had been provided at Mr. Bethune's expense, for one hundred little orphans. They ate up the beef and pies, and thought they should always remember "Peace." In the evening, they rode round to see the illuminations, and as they passed the asylum, gave three times three, which was returned from one hundred little voices within the yard.

When have you seen my sweet sister and her sweet baby? Will you believe me, when I say I do not think much about it, for when I do, I want to see it so much that I banish it from my thoughts?

The clock has just surprised me by striking eleven. I can only add a kind remembrance for all whom you know I love. Best compliments for Mr. Williams, and the love of your affectionate   LYDIA.

LYDIA COIT TO MRS. ELIZABETH COIT.

May, 1815.

MY VERY DEAR SISTER,— Though not at all indebted to you, yet I know you are always happy to get letters, and so

I will improve the present opportunity. I must first say, our dear Sally, with husband and baby, left us this morning. S. C. Day is a charming child, and Sally is a very methodical, good mother. The young lady weighs about twenty-two or twenty-three pounds, is fair and sprightly. I had a letter from sister Lord and her husband a week since. He says he cannot determine what effect the peace will have upon his plans until he visits New York. What amazing revolutions in Europe, — yet nothing respecting that modern wonder and surprise. His has been, and I fear will be, a dreadful work.

This afternoon I have attended a meeting for prayer, which is held by the ladies the first Monday in every month, and is in concert with about thirty, which are held in different towns. It is an animating thought, that at a certain hour (from three to five) there are so many united in asking for an outpouring of the Spirit and a blessing to rest upon the youth. The revival in New Haven was preceded by stated prayer. I heard a letter read from a young man in college, who speaks of W. H. "At supper one evening, it was told that one of his companions had become 'serious.' 'Well,' said William H., 'if *he* is serious all college will be.' 'No,' said his friend, 'we don't even expect it in *you*.' What was said as a jest fastened upon his conscience, and at last he, too, rejoiced in the truth."

We spent a pleasant afternoon at sister Fanning's when Sally was here. Love to Miss Hazard and all who love

     Your affectionate   LYDIA.

Lydia, now being the only unmarried one of the family, divides her time between her different sisters' homes. She writes now from Montezuma, N. Y., where she was staying with Mr. and Mrs. Lord.

LYDIA COIT TO MRS. THOMAS DAY.

MONTEZUMA, *October 9, 1815.*

Will you believe me, dear Sally, I was half offended, when your letter of the 22d arrived to appease my wrath. I had written all my friends since I came out, and from no one had I received an answer. I can say with you, "I am sick of private opportunities," and before I go further I wish to impress it upon you that I shall depend on hearing from you every few weeks; the postage is no consideration when we are three or four hundred miles apart. You ask if I have got the fever and ague? if I have been to Niagara? etc. The first I have not got, and I have added several pounds to my weight since I came. To Niagara I have been, and with Miss Huntley's[1] faculties I could send you a beautiful letter full of descriptions of the terrible, sublime and beautiful; but to you, I am confident, simple facts will be more acceptable.

We left here the 7th of September, and returned after an absence of eleven days. The first day we dined at Geneva, lodged at Canandaigua; dined the next day at Genesee River, and slept at Batavia. The next day we arrived at Buffalo. No town ever surprised me more than that. The first view you have of it is from the top of a hill about two miles out of the town. It is beautifully situated on Lake Erie and the Niagara River, and is now quite a town. Most of the cellars where buildings had been destroyed by the enemy are built upon, and you will know it must appear very new, since they left but one house standing. Cousin George came to see us at evening, and stayed to supper. On Sunday he came and took us to meeting, which was held in a ballroom. The audience appeared very well, and almost all were in the morning of their days, and appeared like young adventurers. G. said it was the case; they had very few middle-aged men among them. General Brown and suite were in town, and

[1] Mrs. Sigourney.

came to meeting. Monday morning, to our grief, it rained, and we feared we should be detained, but happily the clouds began to look favorable, and at twelve o'clock we set out, rejoiced to leave one of the dirtiest, most confused and crowded houses I was ever in. We went first to a large hotel where we were directed; but though wholly unfinished, General B. and suite had possession, and the governor of New York was expected. George said we should have found it worse than where we were. Fortunately for us we preceded his Honor, and, until we got to Buffalo, took the lodgings and meals provided for him. The Seneca Indians had begun to assemble, to meet in council at Buffalo. There is a great deal of dignity in their appearance. We went down to Black Rock, where we crossed into his Majesty's dominions, and went up to Fort Erie, which is on the lake just at the head of the river. Leaving here we pursued our ride on the banks of Niagara River (twenty-one miles) to the falls. The road is beautiful, but the bridges across the creeks are all destroyed, and indeed the fences from Fort Erie almost all the way. At Chippewa we were three miles from the falls, and were all expectation. The vapor had for some time been visible, and the scenery more and more interesting as we advanced. Indeed, I don't know but that I quite as much admired the rapids for two miles above the falls, and the neighborhood which stood tranquil on the shores, though it seemed in evident danger of inundation, as I did the falls. We reached Forsyth's (the only decent house) at dark, and as a great favor were received. They do not keep a public house, and complain of the intrusion of so many people; still, it was apparent they were flattered by being solicited. . It was on this farm that the battle of Bridgewater was fought. When I was being shown up to bed, I asked the landlady if she was there during the battle. She said yes, she left her house and went to a little log-house, where her mother lived, at the end of the garden, during the engagement, which lasted five hours. Two Americans, who were wounded, saw the light, came and asked her for milk; she went with them to the house, and to her amazement, found the floor had been covered with the wounded. The house had not been repaired, and our chamber was made airy by the orifice of a ball which entered and passed through it. In the morning we went to the falls and stayed until dinner, when we returned much fatigued, but amazingly compensated. I cannot attempt to describe what has so often been well done. In the afternoon we were shown the battlefield by Mr. Forsyth, and the *fire* where the dead were burned; five hundred Americans, he said, were left upon the field. Again we went to the falls to take a last view, and then were willing to pursue our journey, which we did the next morning. At Queenstown we stayed an hour, and then crossed to the American side. Fort George and Fort Niagara were in view, but we did not go down to them, as we were determined to take the ridge-road home, and must calculate to get a certain distance to lodge. At Rochester we went to view the falls; they are fine, though but a miniature of those we had seen. This was Friday morning. In the afternoon we had rain; reached East Bloomfield, where we stayed, and from where we had forty-four miles home. Saturday morning was beautiful when we set out, but we found the rain had rendered the turnpike very bad, and three miles beyond Geneva we met with our first accident. The axletree broke, and detained us until four o'clock, so that we were not able to reach home, and stayed at Seneca Falls, nine miles distant. Here we found Governor Gore. He traveled in a chariot, a most foolish thing, not half as comfortable or genteel in my opinion as our wagon; fourteen servants, including housekeeper, handmaid, butler, and two pages. We were amused to see them off, and then started ourselves, and reached home about eleven o'clock. Our horses proved noble travelers, and gave us no trouble after the second morning, when they capered, but were sobered by night, having gone fifty-four miles. In going out we met a gentleman and lady in a stylish wagon, with a beautiful pair of bays and an outrider. When we had passed, [we] found they had stopped, and the servant came to ask if it was Miss Coit, and who should they prove to be but the C.'s. We enjoyed an interview, and found they were going to visit Montezuma. They staid two days, which sister Lord enjoyed. The time has seemed so short that I do not think of leaving my dear friends at present, but should there be good sleighing, I think I should like to improve it, as I do not care to stay through the spring. My cloak is very convenient, and did not exceed fourteen dollars. If you get one, do have it wide enough to lap well in front, it is so much more the thing for comfort. I wish it might be like mine. Next week we will write again, and [I] hope soon to have another from you to gladden the heart of   Your affectionate

LYDIA.

It is no wonder that she wanted to take advantage of good sleighing, to traverse the long stretches of road which lay between her and Norwich.

A year later, when she is again in Montezuma, she writes to a friend: "You ask when I shall return. In the language of the Preacher, I will say, 'When the winter is past, the flowers appear on the earth, the time of singing of birds is come, and the voice of the turtle is heard in the land.'"

We find many most amusing letters about clothes and fashions. Whoever went to New York was expected to "do commissions" for the entire circle of friends in Hartford. A cousin,[1] Miss Mary Ann Coit, who lived in New York, was constantly besieged with

[1] She married, first, Rev. Henry Blatchford, of New York; second, Judge Samuel Hubbard, of Boston.

orders of every sort, from earrings and tortoise-shell combs to stair-carpeting and "jigger irons."

LYDIA COIT TO M. A. COIT.

NORWICH, *April*, 1817.

MY DEAR MARY ANN, — Did you, some weeks since, receive from me a request for a comb? and do you know what a troublesome cousin I prove to my dear New York friends? I really fear they will not love me, I tax them so much. I think of you as exceedingly occupied nowadays, but will you, if linen is what you are looking for, have the kindness to get for me a piece of linen at a dollar a yard? Don't give yourself many steps, — I request you not to. And lastly, will you get me two pair of shoes, one of black morocco, and one cloth, both thin soles : perhaps you will find them ready-made ; if so, I should be very glad of the whole immediately.

Love to your dear parents, and to my naughty cousin Martha, and to my good cousin of the "black cloth,"[1] whom, with you, I hope to have the pleasure of calling cousin in Connecticut. May, I hope you will pardon all this trouble given by   Your affectionate

LYDIA.

We are hardly surprised to read, in a letter written a week or two later to "Mary Ann," that "the shoes unluckily were too large, particularly the morocco ones." The wonder is, rather, why shoes so recklessly ordered should have been expected to fit.

In 1817, Lydia married Mr. Eliphalet Terry, of Hartford, a widower with one child, and her home was within a short distance of her sister Sally's, so that the families of these two sisters became closely

---

[1] Rev. Mr. Blatchford, whom M. A. C. was to marry.

united. Lydia, in writing to Mrs. Lord, in 1819, says: —

As soon as I had taken tea, I went over to Sally's; found her well, and at the tea-table. Her baby has grown finely. I told her I had bought some pretty lace for a cap. Oh, dear, she said, she would dispense with caps, if she could only keep her head combed, and have a cap for the baby fit to be seen. However, she is pleased with my purchase. She should not think I would ever wish to come there again until her children were grown up. She would give me the baby out and out if I would take her. I told Mr. Day if he would draw a writing strong enough to bind her, I would agree to her bargain. He thought he would get a brother lawyer to do that.

Poor grandmother "Sally"! The children came fast, and she was burdened with many cares.

Then come constant references to their intercourse such as: —

Sally and Mr. Day passed last evening with us. She now looks in good health, but has not been out much.

The weather is extreme, and the sleighing poor; but Sally and I think of going, and taking Catherine Augusta, who is a great, quiet, lovely child.

Mr. Day and Sally dined with us; Sally came early, and we chatted busily, if not profitably.

THOMAS DAY TO HIS WIFE.

NEW HAVEN, *October* 9, 1818.

DEAR SARAH, — I arrived here, Wednesday afternoon, between three and four o'clock, and found the town full of election, or something like it. All well at the President's. Noble came in the evening. He has been in the House of

Representatives most of the time to-day. Noble's Henry has been here for two or three weeks; returned to Washington to-day, reluctantly, though without murmuring. I think him a very fine boy.

You will probably have had the news of the ratification of the Constitution. Few of our Hartford people, I believe, thought the majority would be so great. The New Haven people will not acknowledge that they wished to get away our election, or that they are at all gratified with having it. I can see business enough before us to keep me pretty busy through the session. I hope to hear from you often, and let the small folks be the subject; I do not mean exclusively, but extensively. The guns are firing for the new Constitution. The bells have rung to-day as though the town was on fire. Distribute my love to our household.

Affectionately yours,   T. Day.

Dr. Mason, the distinguished theologian, and pastor of the Reformed Presbyterian Church in Cedar Street, New York, seems to have exerted a strong influence upon Lydia's early life. In 1820, she writes to Mrs. Lord:—

A few weeks since, we had the pleasure of a short visit from our greatly respected Dr. Mason. We heard on Friday evening that he was in town, and called on him at Mr. Hudson's. I did not suppose he would have any recollection of me, but he had. He came to dine with us on Saturday, with his son. We had Mr. Day and Sally, and brother Seth Terry, to meet him. He said, had he known he was so near you when he was in Auburn, he should have paid you a visit. He is greatly altered. He said his physicians had formerly mistaken his complaint, but it was now decided that it was a plethora of the brain, and the "doctor dieted him until he could well nigh eat the doctor."

Sally and I thought his countenance expressed more the

simplicity of a little child, than the greatness of intellectual strength.

This same year Mrs. Terry's first child was born, and she writes to Mrs. Lord: —

I must now tell you something of my youngest daughter.[1] She is a sweet little creature, we all think; even Aunt Day says so, who does not love babies. She is said to look very much like me, but her eyes are blue and her complexion fair. I suppose the expression is mine. Her cheeks are very red and she is quite healthy and large enough. Aunt Day thinks her greatest imperfection is being rather too fat. Now by this time, you laugh, and begin to question whether I am not too fond of her. I hope not. I can realize that He who gave has a right to her, and that without His blessing her life will not be a comfort, and without His grace it were better she had never been born. My dear Sarah is happy as possible with a little sister, and is growing into life herself very fast. She and Sarah Day are very intimate, and often amuse me with their conversation and play.

Thursday. — I have just returned from a little ride with sister Sally, her Thomas, and my Mary. She has been to Commencement at Litchfield, and to Norwich. I think she has jaunted about considerably with her great baby Catherine. Take up your pen and devote an evening to me, — do. I want you should write me all about your society and everything of family concern. Your affectionate

LYDIA C. TERRY.

January, 1821.

I have been this afternoon to ride a few miles with Sally and her four. We had a merry party. She and I carried Catherine and Thomas. The two Miss Sarahs and

---

[1] Lydia was a most devoted mother to Mr. Terry's little girl Sarah, and no difference, if felt, was ever expressed in speaking of the children.

little Miss Elizabeth sat forward. Our two families have been in the enjoyment of great health this winter.

February 1.—Mr. Day and Sally have dined with us to-day on a little roast pig. Yours,

L. C. T.

LYDIA COIT TERRY TO MRS. LORD.

March, 1823.

There has been a subject of great interest to us started in the last few months : that of building a new meeting-house and forming a new society. Our congregation is a very large one, and the house, though large, does not accommodate nearly all who apply for seats. Mr. Hawes is so great a favorite that there could be none found willing to leave him. But it was thought by all reflecting men that there was no time to be lost, and after several confidential meetings, a number came to the conclusion that it was their duty to make the sacrifice of leaving their pleasant and profitable situation under Mr. Hawes's ministry, and to open a new house of worship. A meeting was called, committees appointed, etc., etc. The circumstances leading to this are truly interesting. An association was formed a few months ago to build a house for the Universalists, but it was found they were not sufficiently strong, and as a matter of policy, they determine to call a Socinian if they can succeed in getting a house. Such an event was much to be dreaded at any time, but especially while we had no room to offer, and our own place was too strait for us. Forty-five of the male members of Mr. Hawes's church will compose this new society. The object of Mr. Ely's visit to New York is to get a plan, or select one from some church in the city. Hardly any subject has ever tried my feelings as much. I have often felt much satisfaction in the thought of bringing up my children under our dear Mr. Hawes, and of growing old with him, if my life was spared. But we don't know what is before us, and if the path of duty is plain, we ought cheerfully to walk in it. Mr. Hawes called to see me, and seemed to feel much as I did; though the matter, when proposed, met his cordial approbation, yet it has almost made him sick with anxiety, regarding every step as so important. As soon as Dr. Beecher, of Litchfield, heard of the steps we were taking, he was much elated, and came directly to Hartford and did much to encourage the feeble and strengthen the hands that were inclined to hang down. It seems that in the ministers' meetings for some years past, the situation of Hartford has been a subject of much interest. The Episcopal Church, or congregation rather, has grown to a large size from the overflowing of ours, and now we will try and recover some of the stray sheep. But I am dwelling longer on this subject than I ought, forgetting that you cannot feel the same interest in it that I do. My love to your husband when you write. I hope he will not stay late in Savannah.

    Yours affectionately,   LYDIA C. T.

In this way was laid the foundation of the North Church. A great sacrifice could rarely be more richly rewarded, for, though Aunt Lydia did not live herself to benefit by the noble ministry of Rev. Horace Bushnell (who was settled over the North Church in 1833), her children grew up under his faithful care and inspiring teaching.

In 1823 our grandfather moved from North Main Street. Aunt Lydia writes, "Sally expects to leave this neighborhood in a week or ten days. I think we shall both look back upon the season when we lived so near together as a privileged period." One of the children, who was nine years old at the time they moved, gives the following account of that first home:

Perhaps more than any other of the sisters, I can recall the appearance of our first home. We lived in the north half of a double house. It was three stories in height, painted white, with the traditional green blinds, and was shaded by a fine, large elm. In front was the parlor, a room of good size, nearly square, and furnished with a simplicity that would seem very bare in these days of bric-a-brac. Two windows opened upon the main street, and were hung with curtains of white dimity, with a tasseled fringe, which are still in existence. The stiff, uncomfortable sofa was at first covered with dimity, and afterwards with a blue damask silk skirt of Grandmother Coit's. A dozen handsome white and gilt chairs were ranged along the wall like sentinels, and the high white mantel was only ornamented with two pair of silver candlesticks and the snuffer tray, while over the mantel was hung a colored engraving of the passage of the Israelites through the Red Sea, with poor, discomfited Pharaoh and his hosts kicking in dire confusion in the green waters below, while victorious Moses stood safe on the shore. The open hearth, with its brass andirons, gave the only hint of fire for heating this large northwest room. Back of this dismal parlor was the more cheerful dining-room. The fireplace and mantel occupied one side of the room. Two large windows were on another, and under these a broad comfortable sofa covered with chintz. Opposite to the fireplace was the door leading to the kitchen, and in the space between the door and the window stood the large sideboard, still in use. The advent of my brother Thomas, three years and two months younger than myself, recalls a distinct memory of my mother's room; the half-circular tester over the bed hung with a red and brown leafy chintz; the bright wood fire lighting up the shaded room; the cricket or bench on which I sat; and Miss Betsy Smith, the type of all Yankee nurses, who carefully placed the precious boy in my youthful arms. In 1821 my parents united with the Centre Church, and we were all baptized by the Rev. Dr. Hawes. I am afraid the regeneration of this act was not as thorough as it might have been, for I remained a very self-willed child, not at all moved by the influences around me.

There was a clergyman, the Rev. Henry Grew, who held some peculiar religious views. I heard him called a Unitarian, and in reply to my inquiry as to what creed that might be, my mother replied that "they did not believe in the Doxology." As that was sung in church every Sunday, I understood the definition at once.[1]

Our uncle Thomas, in his "Recollections," written at the request of his nephews and nieces, says: —

The view from the rear windows of the Ely house, where we first lived, has remained with me through life. I can see, now, the scows passing under the great bridge, and then putting up their topmasts and setting their topsails, to sail up the river with a southerly wind. Scows, with freight for all towns and villages, to the very headwaters of the Connecticut River, were then fitted out from Hartford; and there being few or no intervening buildings, I could see from our rear windows the whole process. Now, streets and buildings intervene, and the prospect must be cut off. I remember showing one of my cousins, from New Preston, the "Goodwin woods," which were about a quarter of a mile away, and telling him they were almost as far off as Albany. He looked incredulous, and said they did not seem to him so far away. I had a longing to visit those woods, and my nurse had impressed it upon me, that they were a great way off, and that I could not get back the same day if I wandered there. Now, the Goodwin woods are a part of Edwards Street!

The construction of the Worcester, now Boston and Albany, Railroad, was a hard blow to Hartford trade. All the leading merchants were driven out of their early occupations, and compelled to resort to insurance, banking, and manufacturing. Now, with the railroads from the West and South, bringing coal, which nobody then believed could ever come except by the river, very little of the old river trade is left.

[1] Recollections, S. D. H.

I go down to the empty wharves, and see storehouses deserted, and the whole east side of Hartford abandoned for the west.

Aunt Sarah says: —

In 1823, we moved from North Main Street to the Dwight house, in Prospect Street. In the experience of a long life, I cannot recall a more thoroughly good and delightful set of neighbors. Judge Williams, about that time in Congress, and afterwards chief justice of the State, was on the opposite corner; Mr. Ellsworth, on our right hand; Mr. Trumbull (afterwards governor), my father's friend and groomsman, at our left; beyond him, lived our good friend and physician, Dr. Mason Cogswell; and a little farther on, were the houses of Mr. Daniel Wadsworth and his sister, Mrs. General Terry. We moved to Prospect Street in the autumn, and in February, our little brother Robert was born. He lived only a few months, and died, after a short illness, of pneumonia. We children were put into mourning, as was the custom of the time: black canton crêpe dresses, with white capes, and our straw bonnets trimmed with black ribbons. I happen to remember my mother's dress at this time, as I watched her from my schoolroom window. It was black bombazine trimmed to the knees with crêpe, and a crêpe bonnet, and veil which fell to meet the crêpe around the skirt. This deep mourning would be thought extravagant now, but our mother never dressed in extremes, and this was probably only what was customary.

The family lived about three years in the Dwight house.[1] After the death of the infant son mentioned above, a little daughter was born, making the fifth in the group known to our generation as the "Day sisters." Our grandfather at this time was secretary of state (an office he held for twenty-five years), and

[1] Situated on the southeast corner of Prospect and Grove Streets.

also chief justice of the county court, and reporter for the Supreme Court. Thus he was obliged to be frequently away from home. There are a number of letters of about this date, written jointly by the entire family, to their father. In May, 1826, he is in New Haven, and writes as follows: —

THOMAS DAY TO MRS. DAY.

NEW HAVEN, *May* 12, 1826.

MY DEAR WIFE, — I arrived here last Monday, after a very comfortable ride, about five o'clock. Found Dr. Porter at the President's, who was preparing to go on to New York, to attend the religious anniversaries there, and Jere had concluded to go with him. Mr. Lanman is here with his son-in-law, Mr. Hubbard, making interest for a judgeship, or anything else. I fear he will be disappointed. I think our neighbor, Mr. Williams, stands a much better chance than he, and, indeed, a pretty good chance to be made judge. The influence of certain out-door jugglers, otherwise called Lobby Members, will be against him. The old Governor, it was thought, would decline being a candidate for election after this year; but from all I can see and hear, I conclude he does not intend to do any such thing. It is very doubtful whether the party who have hitherto supported him will do so any longer. Mr. Tomlinson, now a member of Congress, is talked of as a successor. The caucus will probably nominate somebody next week.

What will be done with the Secretary remains equally uncertain. It is possible they may allow him more time to be with his wife and children. I am afraid the care of so large a family (for care I know you will take) will retard your recovery. Mrs. Stone and Miss Gray, I have no doubt, will do their parts well; and I hope Sarah and Elizabeth, aye, and all of them, down to black-eyed Hatty, will feel they have something to do. By the way, I have not yet received the promised letter. I inquire in vain at the post-office every day. I hope it will come soon. I want to know how *tiny sister* does, whether she improves, etc. Tell Thomas not to forget the burdocks. I hope to find them scarce in the garden when I come home. The girls will do well to remember that a little water is acceptable to plants in this dry time. My paper is out, and I am tired. Yours,

T. D.

NEW HAVEN, *May* 18, 1826.

MY DEAR WIFE, — I am indebted to you and our eldest daughter for two interesting letters. Sarah has succeeded so well in her first attempt, that I wish she would repeat it.

A very small part, only, of the business of the session has been accomplished. I think the Assembly will not rise before the middle of the week after next. It was my intention to be with you the latter part of this week; and I may be, still. If you should hear a motion of the knocker about twelve o'clock, Friday night, you need not be alarmed; and if you should sleep undisturbed all night, you need not imagine anything worse has happened to me than full employment at New Haven. Papa's love to all the children, whether they have one or two names, or none at all.

Your affectionate THOMAS DAY.

The letter looked for, we suppose to be the following: —

FROM SARAH COIT DAY TO THOMAS DAY.

HARTFORD, *May* 27, 1826.

. . . I proposed to the children, after dinner, to write each a piece for the "Home Gazette." As Thomas's is brief, I will copy it, and leave the remainder of the editorship to the girls.

Mr. Lyman has given up his school, and mamma thought I had best go to Mr. Talcott's. I should be safe there one month, to write, and for arithmetic. Harriet wants me to tell you that she goes over to Mr. Trumbull's new house to "teeter" every day, and mamma expects she will break her bones. Ezekiel has come, and brought up his turtle.

Good-by,   T. M. DAY.

Communicated for the "Home Gazette." Uncle Terry brought down a box full of figs that uncle Samuel sent. They were called Louisiana figs. They are delicious, and mamma took out some, and tied up the box to save for you.

The baby is safe and well. Mrs. Buck has sent up a little cradle, and cushion with life everlasting in it, for the baby to sleep on. From your daughter,

CATHERINE.

DEAR PAPA, — Last night, uncle Terry called and brought a present of figs from uncle Samuel. They are much more delicate than the common fig. The grapevine by the gate, which you trained to the fence, has got about ten clusters of grapes on it. They are now very small, but look promising.

ELIZABETH DAY.

Intelligence Extraordinary! On Thursday, at six o'clock, P. M., a shock was felt here resembling an earthquake, which shook the Court House very much, and perhaps overturned some loose papers in the Secretary's desk!

It proved to be the explosion of some powder mills in Granby.

More news from the garden! The "best grapevine in the world" has about fifteen leaves on it. The Burgundy roses are in bloom, and look very pretty. A grapevine, in the kitchen garden, against the house, is grown so much it will soon want something to keep it on the wall. This is all.

S. C. DAY, 2d.

P. S. *Sunday evening.* — Baby Day is well, and mamma is pretty well.

Mrs. Buck, who sent the "life-everlasting pillow," and showed many other kindnesses at that time to the mother and baby, remembered kindness received in her turn from Grandmother.

Mrs. Buck told me how close and pleasant the ties of friendship were among those neighbors. She remembered, to the close of her long life, a night our mother spent with her when she had a sick child. She described how beautiful Mother looked as she came in, saying the children were all in bed, and she had come to spend the night; how Mother warmed her dress, and then took the baby on a pillow and sat by the fire, tenderly caring for the child, while Mrs. Buck rested quietly, only waking from time to time to see the picture in the firelight, and know that her child was cared for.[1]

In this year (1826) they moved to 48 Prospect St., the house next to the one they then occupied. This was larger, and better suited to their needs in every way. In this house, known as the "Day house," the children grew up and married, one after the other, until the mother was left alone to live out her quiet and solitary days, a vivid contrast to her active and busy past.

[1] Recollections, M. D. E.

PART III.

THE DAY HOUSE IN PROSPECT STREET.

> "Surely Thy sweet and wondrous love
> Shall measure all my days;
> And as it never shall remove,
> So neither shall my praise."
>
> GEORGE HERBERT.

IN the following words, one of the children gives her recollections of the new home: —

I remember well the day we moved into the "Day house," our real home, and the pleasure of carrying in the little stools and other small things. Also I remember that the cook took that time to have hysterics, and lay on a green drugget on the kitchen floor with closed eyes, and that some of the women near said that she could get up if she chose. Poor mamma, it was hard to have that discipline added to the labors of moving! But we did have a happy home in all those long years. I love to recall the big house, and long garden where so much fruit grew, and where Thomas dug artichokes almost before the snow had melted.

The garden, too, was an unceasing pleasure. Papa took great pride in his asparagus bed, and he trained a currant bush that grew there by chance until it was as high as his head, and he was six feet tall. I always smuggled some of my geraniums there, and they grew with a hearty good-will all summer. In June came the lovely damask roses in great quantities. We picked them with the dew upon them, and

they were packed in salt in stone pots until the important day when a neat little colored woman came with her still, and distilled them into the purest rose-water.[1]

Prospect Street ran parallel with the river, and it was only a short distance from the end of the garden to the river banks, which were of course a never-ending source of interest to a boy.

William Ledyard Seymour, an old revolutionary soldier who lost his leg at the Groton Fort in 1781, was a daily companion of mine when we lived in Prospect Street. I owned a flat-bottomed skiff which the old soldier christened "the Commodore's log-trough." I used to run errands for the old cripple. He lived in a little hut on the banks of Park River,[2] and his main occupation was fishing in the Connecticut River. This poor old man, or "Old Bill," as we boys called him, is said by Hollister in his "History of Connecticut" to have had his knee shattered by a musket-ball, and to have been stabbed thirteen times with the bayonet.

I often had to go down to the foot of Ferry Street to buy shad from the boats. They did not know enough to sell them from barrows about the streets, much less from refrigerators in the local market shops. I remember waiting at Ferry Street for boats to arrive. I would look down the river and see them crowding along the shores, and then waited before I bought to get hold of the fresh shad. Good by to the good old times![3]

The father took his children with him often on his "circuit rides." Each one recalls with special pleasure some stage trip. A very fond and loving father he seems to have been. Aunt Hatty says: —

[1] Recollections, H. D. P.
[2] A small tributary of the Connecticut River.
[3] Recollections, T. M. D.

I remember going to Middletown with papa. The stage was nearly full of lawyers, and (what was not common in those days) there was also a Frenchman. He spoke English very imperfectly, but I happened to understand something he said which had puzzled the gentlemen, and interpreted. One of the lawyers said, "Strange that child should understand when we did not." "Oh, no," I cried, "for I don't speak very plain myself." A shout of laughter followed this reasoning.[1]

Another relates that the earliest event she can distinctly recall is "being carried in my father's arms up from the steamboat wharf in the evening on the return from an excursion down the river." Thomas seems to have gone often with his father. A letter dated Litchfield, June 22, 1827, says: —

Thomas took tea at Judge Gould's, and last evening he took tea with Francis Bacon, by special invitation, and had plenty of strawberries at both places. He is a gentleman much more attended to here than his father, who has not been invited out at all.

Thomas himself says: —

I remember that visit to Litchfield very well. I boarded with the judges of the Supreme Court, and remember they chaffed Judge Lanman incessantly. I thought it too bad, as Lanman and Peters were the only Democratic judges, and such men as Daggett and Hosmer and the rest of them were altogether an overmatch for them. I remember that Robert Gould and I made so much noise in the courtroom that all eyes were turned upon us, and I was frightened and immediately left to play outside.[2]

What a liberal education such trips were to grow-

---

[1] Recollections. H. D. P.
[2] Recollections. T. M. D.

ing boys and girls! It is easy to see how closely the father watched the mental and moral development of his children. The home life seems to have been almost ideal. The Sunday evening was an especial time for happy intercourse. The father, often away from home the greater part of the week, rejoices to be again in the midst of his family; many household matters are talked over, a neighbor or relative drops in, and "so the old Puritan Sabbath would soften down to a social happy evening."

Our grandfather was very hospitable, and in a quiet way frequently entertained his friends. One of these gatherings, while the children were still young, is spoken of by Aunt Mary: —

Mother was unweariedly kind and hospitable, and welcomed friends most pleasantly. During one of her larger parties, when I was a very young girl, I remember hearing Mrs. Sigourney remark to a gentleman, "Mrs. Day is looking very well this evening." "Yes," was the reply, "Mrs. Day is a rarely beautiful woman." She had never been anything but "Mother, dear," to me, and so I ran around among the guests until I could see Mother in her soft, grayish brown silk, a ruff of delicate lace about her throat, and a cap of soft tulle. I can see her still, as I saw her that night.

Father's gracious smile, as he looked at his children, often lights up the picture of him in my memory. I recall his coming for me when I was at play under the eyes of some colored servant, and taking me into the parlor to see Mr. and Mrs. Clay. He told me that Mr. Clay would be President by and by, but he was mistaken. It was one of our best means of education to meet the guests at the tables of Uncle Day and our father. The conversation was stimulating, the wit genial and refined.

I remember one occasion when our father explained to

his guests the position he had taken in regard to offering wine. The next day he went to the sideboard, which stood in range with the front door, to take some brandy before dinner, his tablespoon in hand to measure the dose. The door was open, and just at that moment Roger Minot Sherman was passing the house. His quick eye took in the situation at once, and he came in with some laughing remark to join Father. I do not remember the words, but the scene is one of my pictures of memory. The two men were so merry and so courteous.[1]

Education was begun at a very early age in those days. One of our aunts says she remembers being taken to school when she was two years and a half old, and that her mother told the teacher to let her lie down in the middle of the morning if she became sleepy. Another of them says in her recollections that "there were no infant schools in those days," but, as according to her record, she attended three schools before she was ten years of age, we conclude there must have been something very similar. Several of the children went to Miss Emily Rockwell's school. Aunt Catherine says: "When I was not quite ten years old we read 'Comstock's Natural History' aloud as an afternoon exercise, and I got some knowledge of arithmetic, but we had principally a good time and good moral and religious instruction." Another sister says : —

I went to Miss Emily Rockwell's school; she was kindness itself, but I did not learn anything, and spent many mornings in Mrs. Sigourney's grove. Miss Emily would take me sometimes, on Saturdays, to pass the Sabbath on her father's farm at East Windsor. Dr. Rockwell would

[1] Recollections, M. D. E.

drive her in an old-fashioned chaise, and I would sit between them on a stool, feeling much awed as we drove over the long bridge spanning the Connecticut River. I have never forgotten the kindness of the whole family. They made a wonderful cake for breakfast, baked in the coals and cut in pieces like a pie, and I was persuaded it was by far the finest thing ever concocted.[1]

Aunt Mary says: —

From the fact that there were no graded schools, our education seemed to be somewhat desultory, but the formation of character was never lost sight of. My earliest recollection of school, however, is not very pleasant. I was only about three years old, and was punished because I talked with another little girl, and laughed at something one of the boys said. I was sent to sit by the boys as a disgrace. That made the boys laugh and joke, so Miss Helen began to ferule my hand, whereupon I cried out, and my sister Harriet appeared from Miss Emily's room, and said, "Mary, here's your sunbonnet; put it on and go home," and I did. What would be thought of such management now?[2]

Later, all the sisters went to Miss Catherine Beecher's school, or, as it was afterwards called, the Hartford Female Seminary. Their father was for twenty years president of the board of trustees. In June, 1892, a reunion of all the graduates was held in Hartford, and the five surviving Day sisters were able to attend. The eldest, Aunt Sarah, in her seventy-eighth year, was invited to prepare a sketch of Miss Beecher, to be read on the occasion, and we quote the following from her paper: —

Rarely has a school been more richly endowed with

---

[1] Recollections. H. D. P.
[2] Recollections, M. D. E.

teachers, or had those more competent in their several departments. Do not some of those here present recall the names and persons of Miss Brigham, Miss Dutton, Miss Caroline Munger, Miss Frances Strong, Miss Degen, in her French mourning, black and red, Miss Watson, who had forgotten more history than we ever knew, Mrs. Stowe, God bless her, and Mrs. Gammage, whom we liked to tease until Miss Beecher taught us to love and admire her, by telling us her sad history?

Perhaps less progress was made in simple acquisition than in some schools, for I remember certain sad failures on examination days, by girls who should have done better; but we learned some lessons quite as valuable, not always taught thus early. We were led to think out a subject by our own processes; to differ from the text-book, and then defend our position; to strive for mental and moral elevation, rather than to dazzle others by whole pages of dates or figures. These were the standards held up for the education of our young minds.

Yet, in certain studies, unusual progress was made. Mental and Moral Philosophy, Rhetoric, and Logic, were really enjoyed by those who caught the enthusiasm of the teacher. Not agreeing with the views of the Scotch philosophers on the action of the mind, Miss Beecher at once began to write a new Philosophy, found a printer, herself the publisher; and we studied our daily lessons from the proof-sheets, under a strict pledge of secrecy. . . . Long before the gospel of athletics was proclaimed, she had teachers trained in the more graceful calisthenics, and our recess was the time of daily practice. Elocution, too, was a constant exercise; and more than half a century ago the class-rooms resounded with vocal sounds and impassioned shoutings of unutterable aspirates. And far ahead of her time was Miss Beecher's skill in teaching English composition. To gain a knowledge of words, the scholar was taught to transfer poetry into prose, analyze an essay, catch the style of a popular writer, and, if gifted enough, to transmute prose into poetry.

Nor was the training of the moral and religious nature slighted for intellectual pursuits. Many of us here gathered can well remember the anxious entreaties, the earnest appeals, and the wise and affectionate counsel given to those beginning the new life.

We may, perhaps, doubt whether Miss Beecher's Philosophy greatly excelled the one she discarded. But the enthusiasm and thoroughness which carried her through such an undertaking may well have had its effect upon her pupils.

One of the sisters tells us that after leaving Miss Beecher's, at the age of sixteen, she was for a time in New Haven, under Miss Delia Bacon, a person of some distinction. She says: —

Miss Bacon had a class of ten, who read aloud, every morning, History and Mental Philosophy. Once a week, we had a lecture from a Mr. Sheppard, on Conchology. Miss Bacon would question us afterwards, as to how much we had studied, and how much we knew, about one or another subject. One young lady said she knew them all; and Miss Bacon sarcastically congratulated her upon "knowing everything." She was wonderfully interesting, and besides having a great knowledge of Shakespeare, had read many other authors. She was the most stimulating teacher I ever had. She was in her prime at that time.[1]

THOMAS DAY TO MRS. DAY.

NEW MILFORD, *June*, 1829.

MY DEAR WIFE, — I have little more than time to say that I am here, and well. I arrived at New Preston, Thursday, P. M. Betsy had returned from New Haven, and in pretty good health.

[1] Recollections, E. D. S.

After rambling over the hills and dales for two days, I took the stage, last evening, and came to this place; got wet, but not hurt, by a smart shower. Soon after I got under shelter in Booth's tavern, who should greet me but Dr. Abernethy, of Hartford! He is here, it is said, on special business of an interesting nature; and our host thinks there are some indications of a favorable reception. Young, handsome, rich, what powerful charms!

I go to Danbury to breakfast in the morning. I am obliged to conform to stage arrangements. I am well, and

Yours, T. Day.

Norwich, *July* 27, 1829.

My dear Wife, — I arrived at this place, from New London, in the steamboat, Friday afternoon, and expect to take the stage for Brooklyn, to-morrow morning at five o'clock, with an assurance of reaching that place by nine o'clock. My time has passed very pleasantly since I have been here, and, indeed, since I left Hartford; but I have met with nothing of special interest. On Saturday, I dined at Deacon Jabez Huntington's, and took tea at Dr. Ripley's. Mrs. Birge appeared, and was quite cheerful. The three cousin Sarahs are still together, in the full tide of enjoyment. They count fifty calls that they received last week. They must, of course, be pretty busy this week, in returning them. To-day, they are to dine with Cousin Ann Thomas Tracy, and to take tea with Mrs. Joseph Strong.

Sarah Day has received an invitation from Joanna Lanman, to spend next week with her, when the ex-judge and his wife, and all the tribe of Benjamin, will be at Hartford, attending Commencement. I have not been disposed to object, but I told Sarah I would refer the matter to you.

I send a letter to Thomas M., the object of which is to excite some attention to his composition. A little maternal supervision may be quite as useful.

Dr. Ripley has called, to accompany me in climbing one of

the high hills of Bashan, over the river, "to see what we can see." Mr. William Coit, of Catskill, who is here, will be of the party. I shall expect to hear from you by Judge Williams. Papa's love to the children at home.

Yours affectionately, THOMAS DAY.

P. S. — The *grape plants* will need a watering now and then during this dry weather.

NEW LONDON. *July*, 1829.

MY DEAR WIFE, — We have got through with our business in this county, and Judge Williams intends to go to Connecticut River this afternoon. Seven cases have been argued and decided.

You will not forget to send to the post-office and forward to us such letters as you may think I shall want to see. If any come relating merely to business in the secretary's office which Mr. Huntington can attend to, send them to him. Has the draft on Dimock & Marsh been paid? If not, what reason do they assign for non-payment? I have made no calls or visits since I have been here, having been very much occupied with business. I have taken a fine salt bath, and felt much refreshed by it. I shall hope to hear from you by Judge Williams. In haste,

Yours affectionately, THOMAS DAY.

One of the Day sisters says: —

It seems, on looking back, as if the union of my father and mother was almost ideally perfect. Quite different in person and in mind, yet each true helpmeets. Father was six feet in height, with large dark eyes, and hair that curled somewhat. He had a meditative face, grave and dignified. We only expected smiles from him, and a look of displeasure made the deepest impression upon us. He called me "busy idleness," and would often say, "And what is my little pussy good for?" Mamma was small and slight, with a glowing color that lasted through her life; quick to rebuke, but very tender in illness or trouble. Her judgment was almost infallible, and we all learned to trust it. My father would sometimes state a knotty law case to her. Her decision would always be quick, and he would smile and say: "That would be so in equity, but not in law," when she would promptly retort, "Then it *should* be law." My father, though generally grave and quiet, had a strong sense of humor, and we used to know by the slow smile spreading over his face and the merry twinkle in his eye, that something funny was coming from him.

There was a great deal of coming and going in our household. I remember that Dr. Nathaniel W. Taylor, then a celebrated divine, stayed with us, and that I, in usual child fashion, asked him when he was going away. He replied: "To-morrow." On the morrow, as he had not gone, I asked him, "Is not this to-morrow?" and he gravely replied, "My child, to-morrow never comes." "O, then, are you never going away?"[1]

The chronicles of the aunts are full of anecdotes of their child-life, revealing such a happy circle full of mutual love and helpfulness, that one finds it hard to omit anything. At least we must give an account of some of the old servants.

Some of the old colored servants stand out very vividly in my memory. There was stout, fat Emeline, the cook, who made such famous sponge cake and biscuit, that even mamma could not find fault. Oh, how she wielded the long shovel, and brought forth from the recesses of the big brick oven cakes and pies until the tables groaned under the wealth of her good things. But Emeline married Joe Cheat, who was like his name, and a drunkard too, and she took good care of him until he died.

Then there was Nurse Grey, who scrubbed our eyes as

[1] Recollections. H. D. P.

well as our ears with soap. She had little sympathy with children, but took devoted care of us, and sewed nicely. She was quite refined, and mamma always told us we must be considerate of her, as she had "seen better days." I don't think I fully understood what was meant by the phrase.

She had a long hair trunk, with her initials, E. G., on it in brass-headed nails. This she kept carefully locked, and the key fastened to a smooth round shell. When I had been a better child than usual she would sometimes show me a small copy of Goldsmith's poems which she kept in this trunk, and read "Edwin and Angelina" to me. It was after she had read that poem that I made up my mind that she had lost a lover, but even the pity for that did not keep me from plaguing her.

One Christmas Eve mamma had put our presents (Kate's and mine) by the side of the trundle bed on which we slept, with Nurse Grey on a cot near by. It was too dark to see, but of course we *felt* the things and rattled the papers, and made noise enough to wake Nurse Grey. She was boiling with indignation and pushed us back on to the pillows. Kate's head hit the headboard. I had expected to be found fault with, for was I not always sinning? But that Kate, my own darling sister, should be hurt was more than I could stand. I lay quite still, but vengeance was in my heart, and when Nurse Grey's breathing told me she was asleep, I went very quietly to the foot of her bed, untucked the clothes, and with my icy cold fingers tickled her feet. It took long years for me to atone for my wickedness, but as she left her most precious relic, her well-worn Bible, to my oldest child, I think we were friends at last.[1]

After the death of the Rev. Jeremiah Day and his wife, the old parsonage in New Preston was occupied by their son Noble Day, and for many years there was a constant interchange of visits between the two

[1] Recollections, H. D. P.

families of cousins. The "Day house" in Prospect Street was always capable of holding one more.

In the early days there were no railroads, and the "sound of the horn as the stage drove into the street was very inspiriting, and often a loadful of cousins was deposited at our door." No less did the young town children enjoy their trips into the hill country.

When about ten years old, Kate and I made a visit to New Preston. We spent the night on the way at Mr. Frederick Wolcott's, in Litchfield, and Miss Hannah Wolcott came to our room in the gray dawn to say the stage would soon be along. I well remember the beauty of the morning as we took that ride before breakfast to Uncle Day's, our father's early home. The parsonage was large and rambling, well fitted for the large family that grew up in it. A stone wall enclosed the front door-yard. On one side of the front door, upon entering, was the little-used parlor, with the delectable cupboards at the side of the chimney where Aunt Day kept the dainties which her sons loved to send her. The family sitting-room was on the other side of the door, and opened into the big kitchen with an enormous fire-place, where delicious pies and gingerbread flowed forth in one continual stream. In one of the upper back rooms was a loom, and we much enjoyed watching the woman who came to use it.

It was at New Preston that I first went to an evening meeting. The notice was given out in the morning from the pulpit, that there would be a meeting at the schoolhouse at "early candlelight." So, soon after tea, Aunt Day, with her hymn-book and a brass candlestick with a very large base, Kate and I bringing up the rear, started for the schoolhouse, not far from the church. It was all very impressive to me. I well remember a gentleman who told of the earliest efforts that were then being made in New York, in behalf of the sailors, and he fired my heart with a desire to do something for them too. Dr. Bushnell was unmarried then, and at home at his father's, "Squire" Bushnell's. He took us to the "Pinnacle," where there was a most beautiful view, and told us of some of his youthful frolics, which made him seem more like a real man to us, and took away the awe which encompassed him as a clergyman in our young minds.[1]

In September, 1829, the sixth little girl was born (Aunt Ellen), and the family circle was complete.

THOMAS DAY TO ELIZABETH DAY.

NEW HAVEN, *May* 28, 1830.

MY DEAR ELIZABETH, — I thank all concerned for the last number of the "Prospect Street Gazette." I have taken a copy of Mrs. Lincoln's Botany, which I shall send with this letter, for the use of any member of the family willing to study it. The other book contains some useful matter not embraced within the scope of this.

I went to a great party, last evening, where many ladies and gentlemen, of almost all ages from sixteen to sixty, ate, talked, simpered, laughed, and danced, much as they sometimes do in Hartford, only a little better. I came away somewhat after eleven, leaving the greater part of the company moving, as if propelled by steam, down the tide of pleasure. Vanity of vanities! Let us not be so silly in Prospect Street. Among the company, I found Miss Delia Bacon, formerly of Hartford, who was sent for, and went rather reluctantly, I thought, at the early hour of ten, before the display of sweetmeats and confectionery, and when only a few cotillions had been danced. I have a great deal of business to attend to; and, like the story of the bear and the fiddle, must leave off in the middle. You must send me at least one more number of our family gazette. I shall be here a week longer. Love to all. Your affectionate

PAPA.

[1] Recollections. H. D. P.

In March, 1831, Mrs. Lord, who had long been a sufferer, became more seriously ill. It was a great grief to her sisters to be divided from her and unable to give her the care which their sisterly hearts dictated.

L. C. TERRY TO S. C. LORD.

March 11, 1831.

. . . Sister Sally has just sent me up yours of the first of March. How it would comfort me to sit by the bed, smooth the pillows, and hand the nourishment! but that office is assigned to those that are kind and tender, for which I would be truly thankful. May we be submissive to our Heavenly Father's will, and willing to resign life, *health*, and every comfort.

Saturday, 8th. — This morning, I attended the sunrise prayer-meeting, where I met sister Sally, and found she would like to close my letter. My dear sister, I will say to my heart, "Be still." Though you finish your course before us, we shall soon follow; may we be quickened to more watchfulness and activity; we want strong hopes. Dear brother and sister, may you be abundantly comforted.

Affectionately yours, L. C. TERRY.

I avail myself of this little space to assure you, my dear, dear brother and sister, of the feelings of my poor heart. I long to be with you, or to have you with us. Can it not be that you might come by water, and we have the satisfaction of comforting you by our care? I know that you do not want for any kind nursing, yet it is painful to think of the wide distance that separates us; but I reflect that our Heavenly Father is everywhere present with his children, and I am willing to say, "Not my will, but thine be done."

We are all pretty well. Mary is rather more delicate than usual; and to you, I may say, her mind is very tender. She asks many very interesting questions. Last evening, she wished to have prayers with the family before she went to bed, and there is no disguise about such a little one. I look at her sometimes, and think, "Sweet infant pilgrim! you little know how many snares are in the way." But the kind Shepherd will watch all the lambs.

With much affection, SARAH.

Mrs. Lord died in May, 1831, and in September of the same year, the Aunt Lydia, so dearly loved by old and young in the family circle, also died. In writing to Mr. Lord, after her sister's death, Aunt Lydia had said, "Will we not adopt the language of good Mrs. Graham, when her daughter died, and say, 'I give you joy, my darling'?" The same words come to our minds as we think of this sweet, bright, reverent spirit passing on into the fuller and higher life.

Not many weeks before her death, Aunt Lydia wrote in her journal: —

Oh, that I might resign myself with the quietness of a weaned child! My Heavenly Father having given me children whose souls are immortal, I earnestly desire to say unto them, as their understandings open, "Come with me, and I will show you good, for the Lord has spoken good concerning Israel." I desire to assist their dear father in training them up, — comforting their little hearts, supplying their many wants, and teaching them for what end they were created, even to "glorify God, and enjoy him forever." I know well the sorrows of orphanage, and have shared in the fulfillment of the precious promise to the fatherless ones, for which I would bless God.

May I be enabled to commend my husband, and my children, and myself, with sweet serenity, into the care and keeping of One who neither slumbers nor sleeps.

"I remember when Aunt Terry, my mother's sister Lydia, died. My mother walked up and down the room, and sobbed, and leaned on me as I had never known her lean before."[1]

MRS. S. C. DAY TO MRS. L. COIT.

... Yesterday, I took tea at Mr. Terry's for the first time since the Sabbath evening when we took tea there together, after having followed to the grave as kind a sister as ever sisters had to lose. I had dreaded the visit exceedingly; and after I had requested my husband to meet me there, it really seemed as if my heart was seized with trembling, and I fain would have recalled my promise, had I not felt it a call of duty. I stopped to see Mrs. Porter, who is in deep affliction at the death of a sweet little girl of five years old. I then pursued my way; and as I approached the house, I was comforted with the thought that my dear sister was in heaven; and though I should miss her kind greeting and welcome, yet she was infinitely happy. I was comforted with this thought all the evening, and though I missed her all the time, I was able to be, for the most part, quite cheerful.

MRS. L. COIT TO MRS. S. C. DAY.

I do not wonder in the least at your feelings in the call you made at the home of our dear sister. I do not think it is possible for me to have her so constantly in remembrance as you do, as you were in the habit of such daily intercourse; but she has been a living witness for God, and a faithful monitor to me, time after time. I can hardly realize that of the six children of our dear mother, only three are left.

Before leaving these years in which the children are still young, we must make a few more extracts from the "Recollections." Aunt Hatty says: —

I often wonder if there is a house in the land where Thanksgiving Day is looked forward to now with the same pleasure that we then felt for weeks before it came.

[1] Recollections, T. M. D.

One year we dined at Uncle Terry's, and the alternate year his family dined with us. Mother wrote a formal note of invitation to Uncle Terry, and then we children began to talk about it at school. When the great day came, we ate very little breakfast, in order to be as hungry as possible. Thomas cracked the nuts, and we girls polished apples, and had, days before, pounded spices, for it was before the days of adulteration and ground spices. Long rows of pies — squash, apple, and mince — adorned the upper shelves of the pantry, ready not only for ourselves, but for Mamma's poor friends, who were never forgotten.

Fast Day was then kept in Connecticut with great strictness. "All servile labor and vain recreation" were by law forbidden. We went to church, and no dinner was prepared. Papa spent the day in his study, where a bowl of gruel was carried to him; and we children foraged successfully for ourselves in the big pantry. We were allowed to go into the garden, but were cautioned to be "very quiet, and not disturb the neighbors in their reading."

When I went to Boston to live, I was greatly astonished to see how very differently Fast Day was kept there. It was a holiday, not a holy day; people went to drive after church, and had an extra good dinner.[1]

Aunt Mary says: —

The Sunday afternoons at home have always rested in my memory. We were called at five o'clock to the large southeast room, where we found Father seated, with Bible in hand. His selections were generally from the Psalms, but one Sunday I recall his reading, with evident enjoyment of its grand and beautiful diction, the prayer of Solomon at the dedication of the Temple. With Sundays, too, I associate the words from the one hundred and forty-first Psalm, which he used then in his prayer: "Let our prayers come before Thee as incense, and the lifting up of our hands as the evening sacrifice."

[1] Recollections, H. D. P.

After prayers came our simple supper, and then the Sabbath was closed. We might open the piano or read any profitable book, but Mother did not like to have us learn our lessons, or read anything which might dissipate the religious impressions of the day. We were all reserved, as to any expression of religious feeling, in the family, — principle, not emotion, deeds, not words, being the unwritten law of the household. As we grew older, we became accustomed to see our friends on Sabbath evening. Uncle Terry always came in.

I remember a visit I made with Father, in New Haven. We went in the stage, which was already full, as the judges were going to hold court in New Haven; but Father said a "little spider could find room in a crack." As we drove up to Uncle Jeremiah's house, Cousin Martha was standing at the open door. Only the upper half of the door was open (for it was divided in the centre); one small white hand rested on the door, while the other held a book which she was reading. So much absorbed was she, that she did not hear the stage stop, and I saw her for an instant, in the soft twilight, framed by the door. That picture I never forgot; for not long after, the news was brought of her death. She was always very kind to Livy and me, but Livy never could recall her person.[1]

The years are passing rapidly away, and the oldest daughter is now [1833] nineteen years of age, and has taken her place in the social world, sharing with her parents the cares of hospitality, and bearing a large portion of the home duties, while active also in the various benevolent societies in the church and city. Thomas, too, entered college in the fall of 1833, and the household life develops a new phase.

The interchange of visits between Hartford and New Haven and New Preston is incessant, and ap-

[1] Recollections, M. D. E.

parently the cousins are always at one another's homes. In reading the letters written during these years, it requires much familiarity with the different members of the families to realize that Daniel, Charles, and Jerry, so often spoken of, really belong in the home in New Preston; that Livy and Martha and Elizabeth live in New Haven; and Mary, Cate, Elizabeth, and Tom belong in our Prospect Street home, for none of them ever seem to be where they belong.

How happy and bright these years were to them all; how wide-awake and full of interest they themselves were in all that was best in the world about them, their letters plainly show.

SARAH C. DAY TO MRS. DAY.

August 11, 1833.

MY DEAR MAMMA, — Your very acceptable letter, dated from Worcester, was received and joyfully perused. Though I cannot say we are all quite well, yet there is only one on the sick list, and that is Cousin Jeremiah. The day you left he was taken with some symptoms of fever, but through the constant attention of Nurse Grey and the occasional visit of Dr. Bacon, he is much better. Yesterday, soon after your letter was brought in, one was received from Catherine and Harriet; I wish you could see the letter, for we had a hearty laugh over it. Cate wrote in fine spirits; thought New Preston a delightful place, and said that, for a wonder, Harriet had not had a headache since their arrival. Harriet complained that Catherine had told all the news, and that she could only add that Mr. Blake's pig was killed by lightning the Sunday before. You have, perhaps, seen in the papers that the New Preston meeting-house was struck by lightning last Sunday. Cate wrote that Aunt Day told her she never witnessed such a scene of confusion, and Mr. Bushnell (who was preaching) wrote some one here that there was such screaming as he had never heard. I was disappointed at church to-day; we had a Mr. Somebody, or more correctly, a Mr. Nobody, who preached in blank verse. Thomas says he was quite sure it was a quotation from Pope. We think of going to New Haven, Wednesday, if we can get ready. Your affectionate daughter,

S. C. DAY.

In the fall of 1836, Thomas was obliged to leave college on account of an acute bronchial affection, and went to the West Indies for some months. "When in his senior year Thomas went to the West Indies for his health, Kate and I cried ourselves to sleep. It seemed the very ends of the earth to our childish imaginations. Oh, how we watched for tidings, and when, after weeks of patient waiting, Papa returned from the office one evening, and Mamma sprang forward asking for a letter, his only reply was, 'We will have prayers now.' Then he thanked God for the safety of his son, and we knew it was all right, and afterwards read the letter. It was very characteristic of Papa's pious, quiet ways, but my mother's heart has never fully sympathized with his keeping the letter even for an instant from Mamma."[1] Thomas returned in the spring, and was able to resume his studies, graduating with his class in 1837.

CATHERINE A. DAY TO ELIZABETH DAY (AT TROY).

March 19, 1837.

We have just received your very acceptable letter, dear Elizabeth, and I hasten to answer it by this evening's mail. You must be in New York, and ready to come with Sarah as soon as possible, for it is said that *our* river is almost clear

[1] Recollections. H. D. P.

of ice, and the steamboats are to commence running to-morrow. Perhaps you have heard of the sad death of little Lily Bushnell. They have been deeply afflicted. Louisa has been very ill for two or three weeks, but the infant was so well that they scarce thought of that; a week ago yesterday it was seized very violently with lung fever, and died on Sunday. The funeral was attended from the lecture room, on account of Louisa's critical state. The baby was the most beautiful little creature I ever saw; I shall never forget the heavenly expression of its little countenance after death. Mr. Bushnell preached this morning upon afflictions, and appears more lovely than ever. Louisa is now considered much better. . . . A letter came from Thomas, directed to you, which we took the liberty of opening. He still says he is well, but seems quite tired of four months residence on a small island, and says the ghost of old Yale visits him occasionally. We shall expect to see him before the last of April. I wish you could have heard a German or French minister who preached for us a week or two since; he had that pleasing foreign accent and tone that interests everybody. He told a story of a lady in Brussels to whom he gave a New Testament, and she sent him word that she " liked the work very much indeed, and would be glad to see the second number as soon as it was out"! Mary E. says she has given you over, and for my part, I must be candid, and acknowledge that I do not remember what sort of a face you have, or how you look. You do not know how lonely we have been, and are, in Papa's absence; I am sick of telling people what has become of my older sisters, and think you had better come home and speak for yourselves.

Affectionately, Your sister KATE.

SARAH C. DAY TO ELIZABETH DAY.

HARTFORD, *June* 27, 1839.

MY DEAR SISTER, — This week has been rather a busy one for party-goers, for there has been an unusual share of visiting. On Monday we had a small concern at eight o'clock. Last evening Thomas and I represented the family at Mrs. T.'s. The party was small and quite ministerial, and, as is usual there, it was very peculiar. The deacon checked a variety of remarks both wise and witty, by remarking that very few had as many things to be thankful for as ourselves ; besides the pleasures of social intercourse, we had many good things to eat, and then desired Dr. Hawes to ask a blessing. This ceremony performed, we had a very nice tea, and in the evening were asked into the back room, where the deacon made good his word, and spread out a profusion of dainties before us. On our return to the front parlor, Deacon T. proposed that as we had enjoyed so much, we should sing a hymn, and that the ministers might settle it among themselves who should make the prayer. The doctor bowed to Mr. Bushnell, who gave his shoulders a shrug, that told, more than words, that he declined the honor, and so the doctor lined out a hymn, which Mary played, and we all sung. Then came the concluding prayer, and at nearly eleven the meeting broke up. This is a true and faithful account of one of the most remarkable parties I ever attended. . . . Thus I think I have given you a minute account of all that is transpiring in our neighborhood. I can even go farther, and say, with great safety, that everybody in the street has had a cherry pudding this week ; cherries and roses are the staple commodities, and are the coin in which neighborly kindnesses are paid. Old Mrs. Trumbull is here, and Mamma has been enjoying a series of five o'clock visits, such as must have been paid in the year A. D. I. Papa will go to New Haven, Monday or Tuesday, and you will hear from us again there. Past ten o'clock. Good-night. Yours, S. C. Day.

In the spring of 1840 the Connecticut Historical Society met in Hartford. Our grandfather was one of the original members of the society, and in 1839 became its president. A number of members gathered from various parts of the country, and much was done for their entertainment. The president gave a party for them, and it was suddenly proposed to make it an historical party. As many as possible appeared in old-fashioned costumes, and three daughters of the house, Elizabeth, Catherine, and Harriet took part in the masquerade. A gentleman [1] from New York, who was present, published an account of the party in a New York paper. After describing many of the costumes which were worn on the occasion, it continues: —

The usages of society will not allow us to mention the names of the ladies and gentlemen who administered to the gratification of the party by assuming and vividly enacting the characters we have indicated, else we would do so. This part of the fête was indeed a rich accompaniment to the festival, and as it was rather suddenly arranged, it was a source of universal surprise that the illustrations of ancient manners were so perfect. Nor let the modern devotee of fashion think contemptuously of the costumes of the age brought thus to remembrance. We ourselves had no idea, from the old pictures, that those costumes were so beautiful and becoming as we found them to be. And were the ladies who wore them first as accomplished and beautiful as those who displayed them last, we marvel not that our great-grandfathers were enamored of them. One thing more. These pilgrims were not so badly off in the matter of this world's goods as many have imagined, — else their persons could not have been adorned in garments of such costliness, and such richness and beauty of fabric, as those. "Marry, come up!" They came not with staves and leathern girdles, but they had gold-headed canes and money in their purses: and their

---

[1] Colonel Stone.

dames, instead of plain "linsey-woolsey," were clothed in crimson and Tyrian purple, and walked in beauty as the night. But we must close. Peace to them; many thanks to those fair ones who have thus reproduced their fairy forms and brought their names and virtues before us in such sweet and glowing remembrance.

In contrast to the brilliant picture given above, is a homely little incident recalled by one of the sisters in connection with this occasion. Among other guests in the town were a gentleman and his wife from the South. The lady was unable to leave her young infant, but was told that it would be very unsafe for her to bring its nurse, a slave, to the North. So she left the nurse behind, and came to Hartford, hoping to secure some one there to take charge of the child. She found it impossible to do this, however, and was entirely confined to the hotel by the care of it herself. Our grandmother learned of this, and wide open were flung the hospitable doors in Prospect Street, and the strangers were prevailed upon to go there and stay, while the six daughters made light work of caring for the baby.

CATHERINE A. DAY TO ELIZABETH DAY.

HARTFORD, *July*, 1840.

DEAR E., — Papa left yesterday for Haddam, and the house seems unnaturally still and lone, though one would scarcely think that Papa and yourself made all the noise of the family. I believe we have said a hundred times to-day: "How delightful it must be in New London now," and I hope you are using the present tense to express your enjoyment of it. I need not ask what you are doing, for Miss Chappel is always good company, and one does not need to do anything to keep warm such a day as this has been. Mr. Barnard brought the "Dial" here last evening, and it looks mightily interesting; further, I have not proceeded. There is an article signed C. Is it Miss Chappel's? I utterly disclaim it, though it has my initial. Mr. Bushnell preached a fine sermon on Sunday afternoon upon "Influence," carrying out the subject of a few weeks since from the text, "Canst thou bind the sweet influences of the Pleiades." Oh, what a mind he has! He only wants a stronger body to make a wonder.

Thomas has gone to the Tower to-day, at the earnest persuasion of the Tuthills. Miss Bryant, daughter of the poet, is visiting Mrs. Russ, and many of these little parties are made for her. Mamma thinks you had decidedly better come to Norwich next week and make Aunt Coit a little visit with her; she will probably return on Saturday. My letter must be interesting, for it is so natural; like my conversation, — broken and unintelligible. No matter. You understand my infirmities. KATE.

SARAH C. DAY TO HARRIET DAY.

August, 1840.

MY DEAR SISTER, — It seems a long time since we have been favored with any account of your proceedings, but doubt not your conduct has been guided by your *usual prudence* and *discretion*. Papa and Kate left yesterday afternoon for Springfield, and do not expect to return until a fortnight from next Friday. I know you will want to hear all about Kate, and so I will tell you (*entre nous*) that she had a shirred hat of lead-colored muslin, with lace and rose-colored *lisse* rosettes in the inside; upon that she wore a green veil. Her dress was of the loveliest lead-colored merino, the like of which I am sure you never saw; round her neck was a collar of fine muslin, with an open-work and hem, and trimming of valenciennes lace edging; under the collar was a finely plaited silk cravat, with green sprigs upon it. Her hands were incased in a pair of gloves of a yellowish brown, and her feet, in a pair of gaiters of the same hue as her dress. She also bore a bag of twine containing a handkerchief, and purse, and, rumor says, a bottle of iron mixture! Now, won't that do for Kate's share?

Elizabeth has gone on the Hill to stay with Mary Ely, and Thomas is intending to visit New Haven on Saturday; so there will be scarcely enough of us left to find each other.

I would write you news if I had any to record. Everything in Hartford is uncommonly quiet, perhaps because you are away.

You will be interested to hear that Thomas and Wadsworth are to be examined this afternoon for the honor of being attorneys. They were the only ones whose certificates were found regular, three others being refused. They have a lenient set of examiners. Mr. Drake says, "We shall put the screws on." I should not fear that he would be very unkind. Mr. Putnam arrived this noon, oringing Tom a parcel of law books, which have put him in excellent spirits. I am sorry Papa and Kate will just miss him in Boston.

We were glad to hear that you were enjoying yourself so very much, but hope you will be willing to return next week. Bring as many of the cousins as you can induce to come with you. Your affectionate

S. C. DAY.

THOMAS M. DAY TO J. P. PUTNAM.

November 4, 1840.

MY DEAR JOHN, — The election on Monday was very quiet, but an immense vote was thrown, and an immense majority was given, — 783. You may infer that I voted for Harrison, spite of the frauds in New York, and in spite of my "Brownson" taint.

I congratulate you on your admission to the bar, and hope that that ledger of yours will enroll the names of hecatombs of fat clients; from the spirit with which you commence the siege, I cannot but augur success. Read that letter of William Wirt's, in the "Review." It is great, I always think, — so practical, so beautiful, so inspiring, it cannot be republished too often. *There* was a man whom the American nation might have made their President, with credit to both parties. Some of his arguments, reported in Wheaton, to my taste outshine Webster or Pinckney.

I had a pleasant holiday last Tuesday, gunning in West Hartford. Tuthill, Andrews, Comstock, and myself, took a wagon, and guns, etc., and put out into the woods. We found very little game, but the beauty of the adventure consisted in the freedom and independence, and in the delicious state of the atmosphere. Andrews and myself, getting tired towards evening, lay down on the dry leaves in the woods, lighted our cigars, took out our provender, and moralized on the falling leaves ; talked of Brownson and Cousin, and discussed Freewill, Fate, and other metaphysical topics. We might have spent the night in the woods without great inconvenience, but, on the whole, preferred a roof made with hands. Dana's work, "Before the Mast," is in great repute here. We shall see Ed Terry about turkey time. How is it to be with you? I don't exactly like this having different days in different States, but it is difficult to satisfy everybody.

Your friend,   T. M. DAY.

THOMAS M. DAY TO J. P. PUTNAM.

December 23, 1840.

DEAR JOHN, — Harriet has just shown me the outside of a letter from you, received this morning. If you can interest the world at large as much as you do her, the Boston Notion Man would find it for his own interest to engage your ready pen. In answer to your very liberal suggestion as to my coming to Boston, I tender you my most sincere thanks for the good-will therein displayed, but I cannot go. Reflection and experience have convinced me that if I ever do anything, it must be something out of the law line. I am too deaf and too sensitive to desire to practice ; but it gladdens my heart to read what you say about your own prospects. Go ahead, Davy Crockett, for success in the city of Boston is a prize well worth a struggle.

You speak of Brownson, and you think of him much as I do: while I was reading him, I admired without bounds; but now that time has sobered my judgment a little, I am not equally enthusiastic, although I still think him a very remarkable man, and look for his January number of the "Review" with a good deal of interest.

Last evening, we met Mr. Pierpont, of Boston, at a "tea squall." Sarah had some conversation with him on Brownson; he says he knows B. very well; thinks him a very independent man, both in principles and feelings. He admires his style of thinking and writing exceedingly; he spoke of an article on "Transcendentalism," by Brownson, which he said would furnish a rich treat to any one in a sharp, keen-thinking mood of mind. From a lecture which he (Pierpont) delivered here a few weeks since, on "The Practical Man," I inferred that he had studied B.; for his train of thought on the evils of the factory system was very analogous to that which B. has so eloquently expressed.

I like this; it shows that the truth will worm its way into light. "Truth crushed to earth," etc. Is not that a glorious stanza of Bryant's, worth all the rest of his writings? . . . Would that I could hear Mrs. Wood again! The first time I ever saw the inside of a theatre, just as I entered the box door, Mrs. Wood bounded on to the stage, in the "Sonnambula." I heard her again and again in that opera, and each night with increased delight. As this is the 24th, I will wish you a Merry Christmas, though I apprehend you will not get this in season to have the benefit of my wish.

     Yours,   T. M. D.

HARTFORD, *January*, 1841.

DEAR JOHN, — I have been hoping to hear from you, as you promised, and trust you will soon redeem that promise. For the pamphlet on Brownson, I was much obliged. Who is the author? It must be some young lawyer or law student, I conjecture from the style. What do they think of it in Boston? It is argumentative, not abusive, and in that respect differs from anything I had previously seen. I put it into Gardiner's hands, who was much pleased to get it. Perhaps he means to notice it in his review. But Gardiner's present hobby is the Abbé de la Mennais, — the people's own book, which he idolizes. I have read it and am much disappointed in it. But I fear you don't take any interest in the question. If you will read Walsh's recent work, entitled "Distinguished Men of France," you will find what will prove, I think, an interesting sketch of this priest of the 19th century. Your information concerning the railroad dividend proves correct, and the morning's paper contains the annunciation of a dividend of $3 per share. I am going to a railroad meeting to-night, when the Springfield road is to be reported upon, and as it may affect you, I wish you could be there to hear how simply and smoothly and cheaply the engineer will convey you over his paper road. Don't forget your promise to write.

Yours affectionately,   THOMAS M. DAY.

June 29th, 1841.

DEAR JOHN, — How this last week has gone! We are indebted to your friends for more gayety than we have mustered for the last six months. Have met them of late almost every day. Don't you think them rather queer? The black-eyed one talks of architecture, — the Doric, the Gothic and Corinthian, the pure Saxon idiom of Daniel Webster's style, and the *Latinity* of Edward Everett; says that in Boston they pay twelve and a half cents apiece for champagne corks for the purpose of using them to give character to cider bottles; is delicate and timid about taking a gentleman's arm; says she is fresh from school, — ignorant of life, and wants to be corrected if she does anything wrong, etc., etc. Is she trying to hoax the barbarous natives of the Nutmeg State, or is she in fact somewhat green? W., who stopped at her father's house during the Bunker Hill convention, says she is not at all verdant, that it is Boston fashion, and all premeditated. But some of us youngsters differ with him.

When are you to pay us that visit? to leave the dust and chicanery of Court Street and luxuriate in the semi-rural shades of Hartford?

How goes Brownsonianism nowadays? Hereabouts the mania is extending. With myself the freshness is wearing off, and I am falling away from my first love. I still amuse myself, however, in circulating his works. Mary H. is my present patient. She began with the "Dial," and avows great admiration for "Ideals of Everyday Life." She has now agreed to read "Charles Elwood," and in return I am under promise to read Foster's essay on "The Aversion of Men of Taste to Religion." Am I not to be pitied? But it is worth some effort to convert the Dr.'s daughter.

Yours,   T. M. DAY.

HARTFORD, *September* 19, 1841.

It is Sunday afternoon, dear John, and all the inhabitants of this church-going community are in their pews. Everything is so quiet that I cannot help quoting Byron's lines: —

> "So calm, the waters scarcely seem to stray,
> And yet they glide like happiness away;
> All was so still, so soft in earth and air,
> You scarce would start to meet a spirit there."

Remember, man, that I have been smoking my cigar at my chamber window, gazing listlessly on the glassy bit of the Connecticut within sight, the green meadows which border it, and the blue hills which bound my eastern horizon, and then forgive my mawkishness. As a set-off I will suggest that Hartford and New Haven railroad stock is rising. Last Thursday evening I bought ten shares of Mr. Hudson. Next morning, before they were transferred to me, he offered me sixty dollars per share for them, being two dollars per share more than I paid. I mean to hold them at least until the dividend is paid, if I do not make them a permanent investment.

Mr. and Mrs. Seymour set off upon their pilgrimage to the West to-night. Our domestic, Amy, whom you must have frequently encountered at our front door, will blushingly submit herself to the silken bands of matrimony. Our cousins, too, from New Haven and New Preston, who are with us at present, four strong, will soon, I suppose, leave us, and our lonely rooms and shrunken table will suggest, I fear, unpleasant ideas upon mutability, transitory actions, etc.

Wednesday evening. — A tremendous thunder-clap has scarcely yet ceased to reverberate. The lightnings flashed with blinding brilliance just as I dipped my pen in the ink. What is the omen? This is one of those soaking, downpouring rains which Shakespeare had in his mind when he said, "He would not have turned out in such a night his enemy's dog, though he had bit him." It is a capital night to sleep in, and a capital night to write a drowsy epistle. Hartford and New Haven railroad stock has risen to sixty-three, and may go higher yet before November. There is something in a fat dividend, after all, quite pleasing to the stockholder. If we both live long enough, despite our radicalism, incarnations of fat dividends we may become.

Do you and Andrews carry out the studious plan, — Latin, Greek, law, history, French, etc.? If you do, you must be credited largely for perseverance. Write soon, soon, soon.

T. M. DAY.

In 1840, Harriet had become engaged to Mr. John Phelps Putnam, a former resident of Hartford, but who was then settled as a lawyer in Boston. He was a classmate and intimate friend of her brother. On September 7, 1841, Elizabeth married Professor Nathan P. Seymour, and went to reside in Hudson, Ohio, where Mr. Seymour had been called as a professor in Western Reserve College. After this, many letters are written to Mrs. Seymour in the old "Home Gazette" style.

H. DAY TO MRS. E. D. SEYMOUR.

HARTFORD, *September* 23, 1841.

. . . I am sitting at Mamma's west window, and you can fancy how the blue hills look in the distance, with the bright sunlight on them for a moment, and then darkly shaded. We have enjoyed these beautiful days more than usual, in the hope that your journey would be the more delightful. And the evenings, too. Monday evening was glorious, and we were blessed with such an exquisite serenade. We could scarcely enjoy it though, we regretted so much that all our friends had left. The famous two flutes were the performers, and Kate said they never had played with such grace and sweetness. If you long to hear from us as much and impatiently as we do to hear from you, this letter will reach Hudson none too early. What do you think of our keeping a great sheet in the "middle drawer," and writing every night, that you may have all the occurrences? We are thinking of sending Mary next week to New Haven to school. Father thinks it best, but Mother says one has gone and she cannot let another go. The tears start quickly into Ellen's eyes whenever it is mentioned, but we shall try to make her happy. What do you think of the plan? I do not want she should go, and yet have no heart to oppose any effort at gaining a thorough education, for you know how I feel with regard to my own. I have been preserving, working at the business most perseveringly, determined to be accomplished in something. Good-by, my dear sister.

Ever your affectionate HARRIET.

S. C. DAY TO MRS. E. D. SEYMOUR.

And what, dear E., can I add to this long epistle? News, if any has been floating about our good city, has certainly been told before this; as for thoughts, I have not had one for six months. You will know just how I have been employed to-day, when I tell you that Miss Parsons has been

here to-day, and that I have been cutting out a cloak for
Mary, which is now nearly finished. It is an economic cloak,
suited to hard times, being made of Harriet's lead-colored
merino, with a hood lined with blue silk. To-morrow Miss
P. comes to turn Ellen's cloak, and then the children will
be outwardly ready for winter. Are not these interesting
particulars? But when I am away from home I always
want to know what the family wear. We had a pleasant
little visit last week from Mr. and Mrs. Washburn of Worcester. They came to tea, and we invited Mr. and Mrs. Bushnell, Mr. Gallaudet, Judge Williams, and Mr. Barnard. The
evening passed very pleasantly. Mr. Bushnell remarked when
told that Anna H. was to be married, "What, has she cut
her eye teeth?" I am sure he can implore for them most
earnestly that wisdom may be given them, for surely they
need it. Mrs. T[erry] still lingers. The family are calm
and even cheerful, though they expect daily to part with
their mother. I saw Catherine last week, and she was true
to herself, one of the noblest and loveliest of human beings.
Her virtues have been brought out by affliction, like the
writing with invisible ink when exposed to the action of fire.
I must close, though I would gladly run on. Good-night,
dear E., and may God bless you and yours, is the prayer of
Your affectionate   SARAH.

During much of the year 1841, Catherine was quite
ill and Harriet was her devoted nurse. In October
the two went to New Haven to consult Dr. Knight in
regard to Catherine's health.

S. C. DAY TO H. DAY.
October 17, 1841.

On the good old motto that "one good turn deserves another," I have ventured, my dear sister, to trouble Professor
Silliman to take a few letters back to you. We were much
obliged to him and you for the letter of yesterday. Mamma

thinks it will not be safe for you to remain longer in New Haven, as you seem to have fallen in love so rashly with Professor Knight. It must surely be the sympathy of opposites, as night and day are not wont to be in harmony.

Mr. M. preached for Mr. Bushnell this morning, but as I did not feel very well I did not go to church. I escaped the great blessing of a long dull sermon. Mr. Bushnell preached this afternoon, and announced in his blundering way that if his "health would suffer" he would deliver a sermon next Sunday evening on "Prophecy." We may expect something original on the subject at least.

What shall I tell you in the way of news? I know of none worthy of record, for Hartford is stiller than ever. The inhabitants are cleaning their houses, or waiting on dressmakers and having *tight sleeves* made.

What has become of Jerry? We have a letter in safe keeping for him, but fear, if the contents are very important, his interests may suffer. On Friday came a missive for the Corporal,[1] bearing the interesting postmark "Quincy." You know my opinion of love letters, that they should be touched with the tongs only, they are of such an inflammable nature, and I really fear a spontaneous combustion some night.

Do ask Cousin Elizabeth to come up and hear Mr. Bushnell's prophecy sermon. She will have your good company up, our better company here, and Mr. B.'s sermon for the best part of the attraction. It has been still, stiller, stillest since you left, and I can scarcely believe myself the same being that a few weeks since had so many friends about. The very walls long for something to echo.

Ever yours,   S. C. DAY.

S. C. DAY TO MRS. E. D. SEYMOUR.

... Would you like to know what we had for dinner to-day? Mary made a very nice turtle soup and roasted a turkey, and baked some mutton, and boiled potatoes, squash,

---

[1] Cousin Daniel.

and macaroni, and all done on our new range. We did feel sorry to see the crane, from which so many a pot of savory food had hung, taken down, and the old andirons, which had stood from time immemorial, banished to the garret; but *sic transit*, and we think our new friend performs all Mr. Fox, as sponsor, promised for it. Did we write you that Mr. Bushnell was delivering a course of lectures on Prophecy? Mr. Andrews, of Kent, happening in town, Mr. B. pressed him into the service, and he gave us one of his thrilling discourses. My imagination is quite converted, and perhaps my reason will soon follow its guide. Mr. Bushnell was to have lectured last Sunday evening, but gave place to a service at the Centre Church, for the negroes. Thomas, Ellen, and I went over there early, but every nook and corner of the church was filled, and we returned home, having gazed from a distance on those sable beauties. It was a sight to gladden the heart of an abolitionist to see all the beauty and fashion of our good city bowing at the shrine of African popularity.

Hudson seemed very far away from Hartford in those days of slow travel, but it is a pleasant picture which Mrs. Seymour sends (to her brother-in-law to be) of the quiet college town.

MRS. E. D. SEYMOUR TO J. P. PUTNAM.

HUDSON. *January*, 1842.

MY DEAR FRIEND, — It is Saturday evening, and I can fancy you as sitting, as I have been, musing over the week that has passed, and thinking of absent friends. This evening is almost sacred to thoughts of home with me, and though it is not regarded here with New England veneration, yet we live so quietly that I can always secure it free from interruption, and I always devote it to the friends whose converse I would gladly share. I sometimes envy your location so near to Hartford, for at the distance at which we are placed, one day's journey seems absolutely nothing; you can get letters so frequently and so soon, that it seems almost like being at home. Our letters, poor things, have to come slowly dragging along, toiling over the hills in a stage coach; but when once they have reached their destination, they are treated with the greatest attention, — read over and over again to atone for the weary miles they have been obliged to travel. I am spending the winter very quietly, and your sketch of matters and things in Boston opened a new world to me.

I wish I could give you in return a glance at country life; but I hardly know where to begin on a picture that has no striking point, — no figures in the foreground. The village looks like any small New England village, except the colleges; these are situated upon a rising ground a little distance from "the centre." They are large brick buildings, and around them the houses of the professors are clustered. The society is of course limited, but it is very pleasant, and the want of a number of visitors is fully atoned for by the frequent visits of one's friends. Of course there is no opportunity for show in anything, unless it be in libraries, for these are the only things about which any pride is felt. We are roused from our slumbers by the college bell; it calls us to our breakfast, our dinner, and tea, and again it tells us when to go to sleep. Obeying such a ruler, how can we help being orderly? We have books in abundance, and a perfect flood of periodicals, so that we contrive to watch the doings of the great world from this little corner of ours, and though rather late in the day, we see what is going on. A few weeks since I went up to Cleveland and spent a little time with Mrs. Dr. Terry. It was very pleasant, and I saw something of Cleveland, but it is settled so much — I had almost said, so exclusively — by New Englanders, that it can hardly be called a specimen of Western towns. My tidings from home are rather encouraging with respect to Catherine's health. They speak of her as gaining strength and spirit, and I cannot but feel happy. I have envied Harriet the privilege of sitting by her bedside and of ministering to her wants. Harriet is so ardently attached to Catherine, so devotedly attentive to every wish, and so anxious, that I have sometimes feared for her health, but I am glad to hear that it continues very good. This is the first affliction she has ever known, and it is not strange that it should make a deep impression on one whose life has been all sunshine hitherto. It is not strange, then, that it should chasten, mature, and soften a character always affectionate and lovely. I speak with the partiality of a fond sister, but I remember that I am writing to one who is also partial, and I cannot give a stronger proof of my affection, or my confidence in you, than to say that I delight to have this treasure committed to your care. Perhaps I love Harriet the more because I am so much older as to have watched her with affection and solicitude mingled. But I must not go on thus. Good-night, and believe me

Truly yours, ELIZABETH D. SEYMOUR.

H. D. TO E. D. S.

I am sure you would say our dining-room looked pleasantly this winter. We keep fire enough to be cheerful and warm our feet, and the flowers are really outdoing themselves. My red japonica is in blossom; we have two tea-roses, Kate's orange-tree is in blossom, and a little plant of exquisite fragrance, which John Terry brought from Italy. Mrs. Putnam's lemon-tree, taller than my head, is loaded with blossoms, and the wall-flower is in bud, as well as a hyacinth. So you see we have summer even in February.

CATHERINE DAY TO THOMAS M. DAY.

NEW PRESTON, *August* 10, 1842.

MY DEAR TOM, — As Jeremiah has promised to write to Sarah this morning, Harriet and myself have concluded to take the liberty of addressing our communication to you, hoping that you will deign to give it all the attention it deserves, and " due return make."

We had not a drop of rain for our annoyance on Saturday, and reached Harwinton, in fine style, by twelve o'clock; called on Miss Perry, who was somewhat startled to hear her name at the door in such an out of the way place, and just the day after she had reached there. Tarried there until half past two o'clock; the hospitable old minister thanked us for our call, insisted upon Daniel's coming down to partake of their dinner, and almost wondered he did not leave his horse there. We reached Litchfield about five, and after resting more than an hour, an agreeable addition to our party drove up in the stage. Daniel had engaged a good two-horse wagon to be ready for them, and with a driver seated in front on the trunk, Harriet and Putnam looked the very personification of good-nature and contentment on the back seat, enjoying the fine prospects and clear air on these noble hills. Such fleet steeds and good drivers soon found their way to our present habitation, where we found literally the whole family to receive us. Jerry had arrived only about an hour before, and all had travelers' stories to tell. Mr. Putnam concluded to accept Aunt Day's invitation to remain here, so we had quite a houseful. On Sunday Dr. Wheaton preached in the "lower city," and there being no preaching on the Hill, about half a dozen of them went down in the afternoon and marched down the middle aisle, just in time to hear his "finally" pronounced. The dull weather, you will think, has defeated many fair projects, but "the boys" seem to have found time between the showers to accomplish a good deal of riding and climbing. We went yesterday to a most beautiful spot, — Steep Rock, — about two miles from Washington. Have you ever heard of it? We were all amazed to find ourselves in such a place. Daniel thinks the rock must be five or six hundred feet high; it is in the form of a semicircle, at the base of which flows the Shepaug River, encircling a beautiful green hillock; they thought it would be a glorious place for the tournament, and proposed erecting seats all around the sides of the rock for spectators; but this is a place you must see for yourself; no one can describe it. I will leave Harriet to tell you how often our slumbers have been broken by the midnight serenade, and the many day exploits of this lively household. Cousin Daniel is anxious to return through Salisbury, and Canaan, and Norfolk, partly for the sake of the beautiful ride, and partly, must I say it?— to get some cheeses. Please write by return mail. Love to Sarah and Ellen. Affectionately yours, KATE.

On September 21, 1842, Harriet was married, and left the happy home circle.

Wednesday was dear H.'s wedding day. Spent the morning there, to assist in arranging flowers. etc. When I went again at evening, they were just putting on her veil. There she stood for the last time as H. D. She was very calm, and looked most beautifully. Then we descended to the library, where Mr. P. and our groomsmen waited, and we prepared to go into the parlor, — pinned on the white favors, and all was ready. I felt what could not be put into words during the ceremony, and prayed with my whole heart for their happiness in the path in which they should walk. Then came the wedding party, and we were in a crowd of company, while H. met them all with sweet dignity and grace.[1]

These words are taken from the journal of her dear friend and bridesmaid, Miss Mary Hawes, who a year later married Mr. Henry Van Lennep, and went as a missionary to Turkey.

C. A. DAY TO MRS. H. D. PUTNAM.

TUESDAY, September, 1842.

Well! you are my own dear sister Hatty, even though many miles part us, and you shall have a good long letter. I was delighted yesterday with so early and prompt a proof of the affection and good taste in yourself and Mr. P. to

---

[1] *Memoir of Mrs. Mary Van Lennep.*

direct your welcome letter to me. Of course the whole family had the benefit of it, and Thomas was lured to his tea by the promise of the perusal of it afterwards. You must have been ungrateful mortals, if you were not almost too happy in sailing up the North River. I thought much of you yesterday as walking the deck, warmed by the clear, bright sun, and enjoying some of the most beautiful scenes that *I* have ever looked upon, and you could not have thought that I exaggerated the extreme beauty of the Highlands.

Perhaps, though, even in this delight you would occasionally, in a quiet hour, have been glad to rest your eyes upon our home fireside. To describe the scene that ensued the day after you left, would be an impossibility. Suffice it to say that the music of jingling spoons, candlesticks, cake-baskets, saucers, glass dishes, and all sorts of earthenware resounded through our dwelling until a late hour; candlesticks were flying round the neighborhood as on the previous day, and sundry pieces of cake and white ribbon were carried in various directions. We could not weep much for you on that day, lest the tears might moisten the cake, or soil some article we were cleaning, and even Father was heard to congratulate himself that weddings did not come but once a year. Cornelia [Perkins] heard on Saturday morning of the death of her cousin Richard Williams, and Fanny wrote her to return, but her cold was bad on Sunday, and she did not think it quite prudent. To-day, however, she seems quite well. You would have enjoyed as much as I did hearing Jerry and Cornelia try to put each other down. Cousin Lib and I sat by and enjoyed it highly, as you may imagine. Elizabeth, Olivia, and Jerry left yesterday morning, but Charles was prevailed upon to wait for Mary. Cornelia is also going to-morrow, and then, oh, dear! we shall miss you. I am really afraid I shall pour state secrets into some uninitiated ear if I do not soon realize your absence, for I have once or twice turned to say something to you at the table, and found the wrong listener. Mamma continues to keep up

bravely. She has been laying the things in and out of your
box this morning with me, and we fear it will not contain all
you will want. Sarah and Thomas are going to a party at
Mrs. Beach's this evening, but I hope they will find time to
write you before they go. Ellen sends a great deal of love,
but says she has not another word to say; she loves you
dearly, and wishes you both a great deal of happiness, but
she has not anything to say to you. Dear child, she is always sincere, come what may. Thank John truly for his
kind letter. Are you not glad to hear little Horace Bushnell is better, and they feel much encouraged with regard to
his complete recovery? Very affectionately,

From tired KATE.

T. M. DAY TO MRS. H. D. PUTNAM.

October 13. 1842.

... Shall I tell you what we are doing here? It is ten
o'clock, P. M. I am writing at the centre table in the dining-
room. Jerry, Kate, and Sarah are crowding together over a
skillet of water, which is heating at the fire to make boneset.
Ellen is lying quietly, her head in Sarah's lap. The hum
of cheerful small talk between Kate, Sarah, and Jerry is incessant. Your father and mother, as becomes the old people, have retired, and the room bears the aspect of a cheerful
winter's night, — the argand lamp, aided by two of those
bruised tin veterans which your mother has frequently said
she would not allow to come into the dining-room any more,
pouring forth a plenteous flood of light. The scene changes
as I write, and Jerry (invalid, by particular request, for
this occasion only) has been sent off to bed with a smoking
tumbler of boneset, and a teaspoon to stir it with. Would
you believe it, they have urged me to drink up the rem-
nant of the boneset — economical souls; lucky that you are
not here, or you would have to swallow it; the stoutest assev-
erations of robust health would not avail you. The tornado
of parties in Hartford has exhausted itself. We have now

a dead lull, but I scent more fun in the future. We miss you, but I imagine you miss us; so then we are even. I mean to drop in upon you some day; but not yet awhile. I'm much too wary.   Yours,   T. M. D.

Nurse Grey was here a day or two since and wished to be remembered to "Mrs. Putnam" when we wrote. She said, "She appeared beautifully at her wedding." She thought you had an "uncommon maturity of manner for one of your years." Mamma told her you were not a child now as once, but she evidently could hardly believe it. We all thought no one appreciated or enjoyed her invitation and visit more than she seemed to.   KATE.

C. A. D. TO S. C. D.

December 1, 1842.

DEAR SARAH, — We were very glad to receive your letter so promptly on Monday, and now that Mamma has heard from Mary and Harriet, both, this evening, she feels very comfortably, and I presume will not say anything more about letters to come from absent ones for at least two days! Will you think me deranged, or that I am drawing upon my imagination for facts, when I tell you how we all *pushed* up to church Sunday morning against the driving northwester, and gusts of sleet and rain? Mr. Bushnell preached all day and in the evening gave, as Tom said, "a magnificent lecture" on heaven. Last evening being cold and cheerless without, and Thomas complaining of an approaching cold, we concluded to use the efficient preventive of molasses candy with walnuts in it. It was all manufactured and pulled in the breakfast room. He thinks his cold is better, and to-night is varying the prescription by using walnuts and apples. There has been no remarkable change in our home or street since you left. Mrs. Trumbull has not been well, and Mr. T. leaves to-morrow for Washington. Father and Mother were invited to Governor Ellsworth's last evening to meet Mr. and Mrs. W., but only Father had the courage to go.

Now that you have found the way to Norwich, don't forget that the same road leads home. You will probably come on runners; they have been running in our street to-day.

Yours, etc.,   KATE.

S. C. DAY TO MRS. E. D. SEYMOUR.

December 21, 1842.

MY DEAR SISTER, — We have waited day by day, expecting a letter from you, until patience has ceased to be a virtue. We have found various reasons for your silence. Perhaps you are ill, or some of the family; perhaps you are so absorbed in kindly works for your neighbors as to forget your friends at home; perhaps you are immersed in the gayeties (?) of Hudson; perhaps you have taken a literary turn, and intend favoring us with a book instead of a letter; and still another perhaps, and my list is ended, — you may have written and the letter has miscarried. My visit to Norwich was very pleasant, though so full of engagements that I was glad to return to a quiet home, where I stood in no danger of being invited out oftener than once a week, and could not be a belle if I would. Aunt Coit is still the same little, gentle, patient, blue-eyed woman as ever, stilling the discordant elements of her household by her kindness and forbearance. Mr. Bushnell came down while I was there, and delivered his lecture upon "Life." You know he is a great favorite in Norwich. I was regretting after we came home that he should have introduced that illustration of the brown sugar which seems to mar the beauty of the lecture, and Mr. F. defended it on the ground that it was the most interesting thing in the whole to most of the audience, and that he noticed quite a smile of intelligence light up their faces at its recital. I came home a week since, on Monday, in company with Miss Frances Cleveland, who is visiting Mrs. Goodrich, and had a rapid and pleasant journey all the way from Norwich. You will wonder how I can use those terms in connection with such a route, but the road was glazed with ice or a light fall of snow, and we almost flew down the hills, and reached here at three o'clock. In the afternoon Mr. C. Hosmer came in with an "historical gentleman," who proved to be one indeed, — no other than Mr. Bancroft, of Boston. He is far younger and handsomer than I had supposed, appearing only about forty, with black hair and eyes. He delivered the lecture introductory to the Institute course in the evening. Mamma told me to tell E. that "we concluded they were all well, or we should have had double letters." But to tell the truth, her conclusions, as far as I have heard them, are far different, for she has frequently exclaimed, "E. must be sick, or she would have written." You would laugh to see her sometimes come across a well-mended or well-made garment, and hear her say, "Lizzie did that, — dearest child that ever was." Does it not sound like her? If I were only another Franciska, I could tell you all sorts of interesting things about "the neighbors," myself, my "bear," and a hundred other things. If you see the book, I am sure you will enjoy it as much as we have done, and perhaps follow her example, and when you begin housekeeping, begin also a "romance of common life" for your Eastern friends. If you can find a "Bruno" and "ma chère mère" for your story, you will be at little loss for most of the other characters.

T. M. DAY TO MRS. H. D. PUTNAM.

December 25, 1842.

. . . Merry Christmas to you — I wish you were here to echo a response. It seems to me an age since we have heard from Boston. Why don't John write, and why don't you write? If my recollection serves me, you both owe me a letter. Many thanks, however, for the "Transcript," which I received this evening. There is very little here that would be likely to interest you that I can think of. We jog along in the same humdrum way, — now and then a tea-fight, and now and then a party. I went with Cate last night to a Christmas Eve service at St. John's, and to-night she went to hear Bushnell. Wednesday night she is going to Confirmation at St. John's, and Mary Hawes is going with her, and your mother is distracted with fear that she will become an Episcopalian. The times are rife with failures hereabouts. Your father, as usual, has got another note of $3,000 of S.'s to take up. This, he says, completes the list of his customers, and I do devoutly pray that henceforth he will confine his indorsing to his own family, and let other people pay their own debts. Your brother,

T. M. DAY.

S. C. DAY TO MRS. H. D. PUTNAM.

... I did so wish you could have been with us on Thanksgiving Day. We had as pleasant a day as we could with strangers instead of familiar faces at our table and hearth. Mr. Bushnell's sermon was on Labor, its dignity and rewards. Towards the close he spoke of the various plans for social reforms, and, among others, Masonic and Odd Fellows societies. Each man that valued himself and his labor as he ought, should feel above them ; he should save his own fund against the misfortunes of life and its close ; let him stick to his own apron, and not the idle trappings of useless show. We have had a busy orphan asylum meeting this afternoon, and I am tired talking and writing, so no more to-night.

Your loving   S. C. D.

S. C. DAY TO J. P. PUTNAM.

January 12, 1843.

... How do the Bostonians keep New Year's, and what is the latest "notion" on the subject? I thank you most sincerely for your good wishes ; and you cannot doubt they are fully reciprocated. Many thanks for the specimen of Miss Fuller's genius you were so kind as to send me. Contrary to my usual custom, I have committed to memory what I do not understand, and wait patiently and hopefully for the time when the deep meaning contained in the sayings may strike upon my astonished mind. Seriously, if the young lady has friends, I should think they would place her in an asylum; or if the institutions in your vicinity are full, perhaps a vacancy may be found in our Retreat. Mr. Lord is here now delivering his course of lectures, and they are well attended and very generally admired. Whatever may be said of the lectures, there is no doubt that the lecturer is in every sense of the word an original. We are intending to invite him here to-morrow evening. I anticipate quite a treat, as he is represented to be very amusing in private life. It is always a treat to come in contact with *characters*, as the distinctive lines in most have been carefully erased by education and habit. I have been much engaged the past week in reading a sober book translated from the German of De Wette, entitled "Practical Ethics, or Human Life." It treats of character in its highest sense, and is so rich in truth, and so full of glowing illustration, that it is delightful reading, as well as profitable. It is edited by Dr. Ripley, and is transcendental in its best sense, and has not one word of the cant that is sometimes so offensive in their writings. I remember Mr. Bushnell says in one of his sermons, "that it is better to try to understand one thing that we cannot, than to contemplate a dozen things that are familiar to our minds." I fear that my letter has been written in such haste that you will have the full benefit of trying to make some sense out of what has no meaning.

Your affectionate sister,   S. C. DAY.

S. C. DAY TO MRS. H. D. PUTNAM.

February 24, 1843.

MY DEAR HARRIET, — Let me tell you how busy we have been to-day, and then you will admit that our plea of having been too busy to write is a sincere one. You know well the usual occupations of a cold winter's morning: breakfast late, and Thomas still later; then Ellen bundled off to school, fearing each moment that she will be late. After dusting the parlor I sat down to worsted work, and Kate to writing for Papa. At eleven we went up to dress to make some calls, but I was called down to see a "tall lady and gentleman," who proved to be H[arriet] Ellsworth and her brother Oliver. Then in came Mr. Watkinson, for Russell's "Modern Europe." Next, Mrs. Daniel Wadsworth stopped in her double sleigh to know if we would ride, and as the morning was fine we accepted the invitation. On our return we stopped at Mr. Wadsworth's to see H. Silliman a little while. After dinner we went out on the Hill to make our calls. . . . I should like your assistance in playing a joke upon M. H. to pay her for sundry ones upon me. When she was in Boston she was very much interested in Dr. Howe and that set of people, and passes for a philanthropist among them. Now I want to ask you or Mr. P. to direct some newspaper or pamphlet to her, no matter for the subject, — common schools, paupers, insane, or blind, — but get some one else to direct it, that if she should show it to me I may not recognize the handwriting. Any legislative document will do if it pertains to such topics. . . . Mr. Bushnell preached on Sunday evening on "Waiting upon God," and accounted for the peculiar state of things among us by saying that we had relied too much upon means, and God would have His people learn to wait on Him. He hoped after this we should "hear no more of winter religion and summer cessation, and above all of getting up a revival."

We learn from good authority that "Mr. Putnam has argued a case in the Supreme Court, and appeared very well;" so we wish you both joy. All things must end, and so my letter, with the love of all.   Yours ever,

S. C. D.

S. C. DAY TO MRS. H. D. PUTNAM.

February 25, 1843.

Mr. Bushnell is going to preach Mr. Towne's installation sermon, and if it is as soul-stirring as the one he has given us this eve on Puritanism, it will surely be worth hearing. The church was densely crowded, even to the aisles in the galleries, and the sermon closed by Mr. B.'s reciting the last verse of "The church without a bishop," etc. Immediately the organ struck up, the choir rose, and the audience rose, too, while we had the other verses well sung. I assure you, I feared the church would next ring with cheers for the Puritans and their defenders. A solemn blessing closed the services, and the great number dispersed quietly. We overheard a strange lady say that it was a great intellectual treat to hear Mr. B., and thought her a sensible woman. Mr. Bushnell will probably be in Boston next week.

S. C. D.

S. C. DAY TO MRS. H. D. PUTNAM.

March, 1843.

MY DEAR HARRIET, — I have seated myself to scrawl a few lines to you. And first let me thank you for the letter and parcel by Mr. Forbes, which came safely. We can see no defects in the "mark," and think it very pretty. Thomas seems inclined to adopt it for his prayer-book, and, indeed, I am inclined to think so young a novitiate finds it difficult sometimes to keep his place. Who do you think we had to lecture last evening? Even Ralph Waldo himself, with his beautiful smile and rich sweet voice. His subject was "Domestic Life," and it really vexed my righteous soul that so few could appreciate its beauty. He had two auditors whom every one was surprised to see there — no other than the Chief Justice and his lady, who came, no doubt, to see that nothing wrong was said in that lecture room. Cousin M. was here the day before, and when I asked her if she were

going, said decidedly, "No," and went on about the perniciousness of such doctrines, the danger of handling pitch, etc., etc. I felt in a teasing mood, and took the essays from the table to show her how they were thumbed and marked, and what indubitable evidence they gave of being often read, and even went so far as to read some passages from the "wicked book." What changed her mind I know not, but I believe she threw it upon the judge, and said he thought he should like to hear Mr. Emerson. If we may take this as a fair sample, I should not think Mr. Emerson superior to Mr. Bushnell in vigor or originality, but he has more grace and fascination, and a manner that is extremely taking. All last week my throat and lungs were very sore, and Sunday and Monday I was ill from medicine that Dr. Fuller and Mamma contrived to put down my innocent throat. I had breakfasted in my room Tuesday, when Kate brought up the paper which announced Mr. Emerson's lecture. Immediately I began to improve, came downstairs, and Wednesday evening went to the lecture without hurt or detriment, so that I can recommend Transcendentalism as a sovereign cure for sore throat and affections of the lungs, and equally useful for any weakness of the head. If these doctrines could be made into pills, I would subscribe a certificate with all due form as to their usefulness. I must close, for time and paper are about exhausted; but to any of my sisters I could scribble all night. Thomas sits "spouting" by me, having taken up a sermon on which to practice his oratory. All the rest have retired. Again, I must say good-night to you both.   From your affectionate
S. C. DAY.

C. A. DAY TO J. P. PUTNAM.

March 25, 1843.

MY DEAR MR. PUTNAM, — I was so much alarmed at the reception of a notice from a Justice of the Peace, and so much impressed with the honor imposed upon me, that I trust you will forgive all appearance of mental distraction in this reply. . . . Perhaps you may remember with some pleasant associations (I am sure H. will) the seat I now occupy. The parlor being somewhat cool, and the breakfast-room table crowded with a group of readers and talkers, I have retired to the ottoman in the corner of the little front hall, where I can enjoy the full warmth of the old Nott stove, and better still, a little retirement. Half hidden by the cloaks and wrappers hanging above and around me, and the little table upon which you have played so many games of chess before me, I can indulge in reminiscences of the scenes of bygone hours, and the many little transactions to which this hall could be a witness. How many times have we sat here till we were perfectly baked, to finish some interesting conversation, but ostensibly for the purpose of getting warm. How much I should like to know how you are both occupied this evening. The Rev. Mr. Giles, of your good city, has delivered one eloquent lecture here, and promises another this week. His delineations of Irish character are to the life. You must give Hatty the most appropriate half of this letter, for as philosophers assert that the smallest particles of matter are divisible, so perhaps this infinitesimal particle of mind may be. My letters to you are always for her, but she must use her discretion in betraying hers to your knowing eye. Affectionately,

C. A. D.

M. F. DAY TO MRS. H. D. PUTNAM.

May, 1843.

DEAR HATTY, — Livy was at first quite disconsolate that you should leave her, and felt quite lonely, but Sunday evening she said it was quite pleasant even without Hatty. She left us yesterday morning. All the useful people are so tired with house-cleaning that they are e'en forced to make me their scribe. Mother is quite glad that Father intends prolonging his stay with you, as he seems to be enjoying himself so well, but her private reason is that she will have a longer house-cleaning jubilee. Mr. Averill, of Salisbury, called here yesterday to see Father. He said that he was the teacher of Father and Uncle Mills when he lived in New Preston, but he had left there forty years ago. He regretted very much that he could not see Papa; said he "had reckoned a good deal on seeing Mr. Day." Kate was quite delighted to see him, he looked so fresh and hearty, yet he said he was seventy-three. He asked innumerable questions about Papa, even as to whether he had improved in point of flesh. Mr. Bushnell gave us a sermon on wearing ourselves out; he said that nine tenths rusted out, while one tenth wore out, — that the problem of life was not how long to live, but how much. Thomas insisted upon it that it was an extraordinary sermon even for Mr. B., but Kate said he had been used to potatoes so long that meat seemed very strong. Mr. B. said, "Let me die by flood, or fire, or the knout, — but I pray that I may never rust out." Thomas has gone to the Polemic which meets at Mr. Hamersley's. My love to Father and Mr. Putnam. Yours in haste,

MARY.

To all to whom these Presents come. Greeting:
HUDSON, *December* 20, 1843.

MY DEAR MOTHER, — What shall I say for joy, except that Elizabeth has a son! A real live little boy, "stout and hearty," Mr. Seymour says with his face all one great smile, such as he has not worn, at least for two or three days. And Elizabeth is comfortable. This is all I can say to-night, for I am trembling all over from excitement. In the morning I will give you a fuller account, but my first thought was of you.

Thursday. — All has gone well. The young Professor has certainly given good evidence of being alive and having good strong lungs. Mr. Seymour charges me with calling him a little monkey first, and then saying that he looked just like him. Now what shall be the name of this youth, is the next question to be settled. We did want so much to call it Catherine, but alas for the feminine termination! and now I think it will be Charles. Have you finished reading the long letter I sent you on Monday? Yours has been read and re-read a great many times. You will find in the last "Ohio Observer" an article of Mr. Barrows upon the Liturgy Article in "The New Englander." We were so much excited by that, that we all wanted to write something. I agree with Mr. Cox that the Liturgy is in no danger from such attacks. Love to all from all,

Your affectionate daughter,   C.

S. C. DAY TO MRS. E. D. SEYMOUR.

HARTFORD, *February* 27, 1844.

MY DEAR SISTER, — Your letter reached us in the midst of no common doings, I assure you, for we were in the full tide of convention glory, with a house full of good whigs and true. We were very busy, early in the week, making cake and pies, and Wednesday morning Mamma and I ransacked every blanket-closet and drawer for bedding. We arranged the vacant rooms, and then sat down to await events. First came John Boswell, one of a numerous delegation from Norwich. Then our neighbor, Mr. Goodrich, brought in two whigs and introduced them as Mr. H. and Mr. S., from Norfolk. Then came "Sister" Northrop to make a call, and Mother, in the plenitude of her generosity and hospitality, invited him to stay with us, — an offer readily accepted. Then came another Norfolk whig, and our numbers were arranged for that night. The next morning was gloriously fine. The sun unclouded, the heavens the deepest blue, and the air as mild as May. Mary and I went over to the Atheneum and the Historical Room to see them swarm up from the railroad. When we returned, morning callers began to pour in; Mr. George Ripley, Mr. Jonathan Trumbull, Henry Ward, Mr. Gardiner (who was accidentally in town), etc. Mr. S. dined with us, and Dr. Pearson, of Windsor, with a young Mr. Beckly ; these, with our five delegates and our family, made our table full. Conversation was very animated, as Mr. Gardiner did excellent execution with his tongue, and differed from John Boswell on some question of state policy, which was a great help. Our country friends looked in perfect agonies if a word was addressed to them, but they liked to listen. Mother almost lost her patience with them, good whigs as they were, because they were so stupid at table. You know her horror on that subject.

At four o'clock we went over to Lawyer Ely's office to see the crowd and hear the speeches. The air was so mild we could sit with perfect comfort by open windows, and we were near enough to catch crumbs occasionally. Perhaps it was as much as poor ignorant woman could digest. Judge and Mrs. Hubbard, Judge and Mrs. Williams, and Henry Hubbard and Mr. Bushnell joined us, so that we had a very pleasant time. We had reserved our parlor chamber for Mr. Foster, of Norwich, who was expected, hour by hour, from New London, where he was attending court; but as he did not come, Thomas went over to Union Hall to see if there were any more unprovided with lodging. Soon after he left, Editor Boswell came in with four men, to know if they could be accommodated. I gave them a welcome, though they were only introduced as "members from Colchester." In a few minutes Tom came with three more. Mamma and I put our wits to work to arrange for them. One cot-bed was pulled to pieces to make two ; a feather bed was put on the library sofa for one man, and a mattress on a lounge for two little ones. I had the want of patriotism to lock the china-closet door, but nothing was missing in the morning except ten of the men, who left before breakfast. So ends the history of the Hartford Convention, and no doubt you are tired of it. Mary Ely says she miscalled all their delegates, but she told Lottie they would think she was cross-eyed, and saw one when she spoke to the other.

Many kisses for that dear baby. What does he wear, and how does he sleep? tell us all about him; and with much love to all, I am his aunt and   Your affectionate

SARAH.

S. C. DAY TO MRS. E. D. SEYMOUR.

April 28, 1844.

MY DEAR SISTER, — We gladly improve the opportunity afforded by the return of your village Rothschild to tell you how surprised and delighted we were to see Cate, how she is, and all things big and little that interest us and will interest you. I am sorry to hear, from your letter and Cate's representations, that Mary is making you so much trouble.

We have become really much attached to *our* little Mary, and could not keep house without her. I can tell you a little how we managed with her, which may be some comfort and assistance to you in worrying with your Mary. You know that she was sent to Mrs. Sherman, and then to Mrs. Lathrop, and returned from both places as an incorrigible liar and thief, and very artful, — no very tempting character, to begin with, — and mamma thought it useless to make any attempt to keep her. But we knew not what to do with her, and I was full of hope, and she stayed. I first made her feel that I was her especial friend, and then set about converting her two great faults. I gave her for each a showering with cold water at different times, to impress her fully with the idea that sin and sorrow are indissolubly connected, and then held up to her the enormity of her two faults, as opportunity offered. I read her the story of Ananias and Sapphira, but she evidently reasoned that she had told a great many lies, and was alive yet. She knows not the meaning of the word "pilfer," and her system of theology is very short. Stealing and lying are linked. For months, now, I do not know that she has taken anything that was not her own, and she appears cured, though the sins may break out again.

You have a great hold on your Mary in her fondness for the baby, and I should try to impress her with the thought that she must be to him as an elder sister, to teach him everything that is good. It will afford you an excellent opportunity of acquiring, in your management of her, that firmness, tact, and quickness of attention that children demand. Many of the little girls we have put out have required a thorough breaking-in, and sometimes the ladies have thought they must return them, but by steadily overcoming evil with good, they have succeeded, and found the children invaluable servants. Make her feel that your spirit is a good one, and that it is the master spirit. Their impressibility is one of the most wonderful features of their characters. It is not at one cutting that the beautiful image is hewn out of the rough marble, but the patient and enthusiastic artist chisels long and patiently at his task. If you have not hope that her faults will be cured, she will find it out, and her efforts at improvement will be in proportion to your earnest hope. I have been quite an education-martyr for a few weeks, and I feel entitled to speak warmly. For two years I have been determined that our orphan boys should have a good school, and last fall the town gave us $150 salary for a first-rate teacher. The ladies of our board are completely managed by Mr. H., and have yielded to his desire that they should employ a girl who has been employed as a servant in his family this winter. He claims high wages for her. Mr. H. has abused me plentifully, and the ladies who are opposed to me on the board make no ceremony of saying rather unkind things. Still I know that I am in the right, and that in time the others will lead up to my notions. My pen has moved at double-quick time, and I have not said half I wanted to. We shall hope to hear from you very soon. With many kisses to little Charlie, As ever, yours,

S. C. Day.

P. S. — Mr. Bushnell took tea here Sunday evening; he said that if he were a member of the Ohio legislature, the first thing he would vote for would be a mountain, and he said he knew now why the pyramids of Egypt were built, — they wanted something to look at.

S. C. DAY TO MRS. H. D. PUTNAM.

April, 1844.

. . . Thomas heard that your good husband was, or had become, a "liberty party man." Please give him my kindest love, and assure him that I will never think of him or speak to him again if he becomes an Abolitionist or joins that detestable party. "Locofocoism" is out and out wicked, and therefore has the respectability that decision gives, and you know where to find and how to avoid it; but I would ten times rather be a monarchist than a "liberty party man."

Mr. Bushnell preached a sermon on Fast Day, which gave terrible offense. Mr. G. would not come to church all last Sunday, he was so shocked at it, and Uncle Terry thought of going out of church, and of course Mr. J. P. Brace would have been obliged to follow, and, worst of all, L. pronounced it impudent and impertinent! It was on the abuse of the elective power, and that we had no right to choose the least of two moral evils. "We may not choose between Sodom and Gomorrah;" "we may not take six instead of seven devils." Ellen has gone to spend the day with Emily Perkins, and I hope she will be rejuvenated, for study and spring weather have made her quite an antique. We expect Livy the last of next week, and she will stay a month or six weeks. In haste for the mail.   Yours,   S. C. D.

C. A. DAY TO MRS. H. D. PUTNAM.

May, 1844.

. . . We have had Mr. Bushnell to-day. It was his first appearance since Fast Day, and I presume he has lost no real friends. He was at home a few days before his wife, and was engaged for every meal beforehand. He took tea here Friday eve. Ask John what he means by being a "liberty party man;" we could not make it out, — whether he would really vote against Henry Clay.   Affectionately,

CATE.

S. C. DAY TO MRS. H. D. PUTNAM.

June, 1844.

MY DEAR SISTER, — You may well believe that your welcome hand was more than ever welcome this evening. As you may imagine from Mamma's census of our household, we have a merry time, and the sounds of singing and laughter make the walls of 15 [1] Prospect Street reëcho as of old. Our visit to New Haven was pleasant to the last moment. The girls heard Ole Bull in New Haven on Tuesday, and on Friday, Cate, Thomas and I had the exquisite pleasure — such I must indeed call it, though it may seem too much like a cant phrase to convey all I intend to express. Mr. Bushnell sat with us, and was perfectly delighted. Many were there from fifteen or twenty miles away; so to say that the Yankees love music better than their dollars, is to state a simple fact. Mr. Bushnell has given us two fine sermons to-day directly combating Unitarianism, especially a tract that they have put in circulation here. With much love to all, from all, As ever, your affectionate

S. C. DAY.

T. M. DAY TO J. P. PUTNAM.

DEAR JOHN, — In regard to your New Haven Railroad stock, my advice is to hold on. The road will soon be united with the Harlem road, and the chain between New York and Boston complete. Beware, at least, how you trust the gentleman you mentioned; his fortunes are desperate. He cannot get credit for a dollar here. Utter ruin is at his heels. I believe the road will reach par before long. Judge, then, what a fool I was to sell at fifty-eight. But live and learn. The state is wide-awake in politics. Send home anybody that can vote for Baldwin. Every man will be wanted.

Yours, T. M. DAY.

---

[1] A few years later the number of the house was changed to 48.

S. C. D. TO H. D. AND J. P. PUTNAM.

January 1, 1845.

The first date of this new year shall be yours, my dear sister and brother, and the sincerest wishes that the year may be to you indeed a "happy" one. I can scarcely realize that but two days have passed since I kissed little Kate and bade you adieu. I flatter myself a letter from the runaway will be acceptable. As all travelers do, I will begin with an account of my long, tedious, hazardous, and eventful journey. The cars moved on at their usual pace until we reached Springfield at half past seven o'clock. I insisted upon having my window open, for which everybody looked daggers at me, and thought I was bent on self-destruction. At eight we took the cars for Hartford, and please tell Rebecca that they are the luxury of motion. I thought I should feel "pokerish" on crossing that frightful bridge, but so great was my joy to see again the blue waters of the Connecticut, which rolled on as freely as at midsummer, that all my fears vanished like the waste steam of the locomotive. Soon after the Centre Church bell had tolled out the hour for retiring,[1] we were landed safely in Prospect Street. A nice little oyster supper was awaiting our arrival, to which we did ample justice.

The road between Springfield and Hartford had only recently been finished, and in the early days of railroading, undoubtedly it did seem a little "pokerish" to trust oneself on the long bridge which spans the river. But there was much rejoicing at both ends of the line that steam could take them all the distance which for so long had been eked out by stage and boat.

[1] Nine o'clock.

S. C. D. TO H. D. P.

January 11, 1845.

MY DEAR HARRIET, — Last evening, Mamma had her chosen circle to tea at six o'clock (the fashionable hour here now) — all the Terrys, Collins, Aunt Ely and Mary, Miss Apthorp, Mr. Bushnell, and our neighbors, etc., etc. There is a visiting fever here now, and if I can find an evening next week, I hope to have a party of all to whom we are indebted. So much for social affairs. What do you think Mr. Bushnell has taken up now? Last Sunday morning he invited his people all to come in the afternoon and hear what they were all interested to know. Every one went, and the subject announced was "The Church Debt." He was even eloquent upon this most unpropitious theme, and those who began to listen in wonder ended in tears. He said that he had conferred with no one on the subject; but Deacon Collins met him at the door with a pledge for $1,000 for himself, and a promise of personal aid. Mr. Collins said that his mind had been drawn to the subject since the morning service, and at noon he decided on the amount of his subscription, and resolved to throw himself into the work if he broke his neck. Three thousand out of the ten thousand needed are already secured, and we hope the plan will succeed, and the deacon's neck be saved for more usefulness. Thomas has just come in to dinner, and says that John has gained his case. Please give him my sincere congratulations if his client deserved to escape; if not, I fear his eloquence was worse than thrown away. Please inclose little Cate in a bundle, and send on. I will pay freight. Ever affectionately,

S. C. DAY.

Sabbath evening. — We have been to church this afternoon, my dear Harriet, to receive Mr. Bushnell's parting counsel and blessing before he goes across the waters. He was simple, straightforward, and affectionate, and if any of the numerous throng that filled the church from mere curiosity were disappointed, they richly deserved it. I cannot write to-night. I feel sober and sad, for Mr. Bushnell said some things that came home to me with peculiar force.

Yours,   KATE.

S. C. DAY TO MRS. H. D. PUTNAM.

SABBATH EVE, *October*, 1845.

MY DEAR SISTER, — We have had a rather dissipated Sunday evening thus far, as Mr. Hastings came over to tea, and Dr. Taft has just left, after one of his long calls. The rain is falling without, and its dropping only varied by the chime of the church bells calling out the faithful few this wet evening. We have been thinking and talking a good deal about hydropathy, and Cate finally desired Dr. Taft to write to Dr. Wesselhoeft to know if she could be received at Brattleboro'. If his answer should be favorable, we shall probably start very soon, and the next thing you will hear from us, perhaps, will be that we are half drowned under the douche of a mountain torrent. I shall ask for only one bath daily, but Cate will come under the full blast of treatment. She has excellent courage about going, and wishes we could start to-morrow. Oh, I have an engagement to tell you; a real *bona fide* one, and made by a much surer match-maker than Mme. Rumor. The parties are Miss H. E. and Rev. Mr. C. Cate says she sees "that great forefinger of Dr. Hawes in the matter quite as plainly as the finger of Providence." Mr. Perkins came for me Thursday to go out and spend the night, that I might meet Mr. and Mrs. Stowe. The visit was a perfect little gem of a time, for the weather and scenery were delightful out of doors, and the company no less so within. The next morning we all came in, in the "carry-all," and left the learned professor with his learned wife at the cars to start for Boston. They will be at Mrs. Greely's, in Cambridge Street, and would be glad to see you if you can call.

Affectionately,
S. C. D.

In the fall of 1845 it was decided that Catherine, who had long been a sufferer from nervous dyspepsia and kindred ailments, should go to Brattleboro' to try the water cure, which was just then at about the high-water mark of its celebrity. Sarah accompanied her, and stayed until the latter part of February, 1846. After her return to Hartford she writes the following letters to Kate. There had been a heavy fall of snow, which detained her on the journey.

February, 1846.

. . . We waited patiently as we could at Springfield, until it became apparent that there was no going before dinner, and resigned ourselves to our fate. Travelers came in at half past eleven, who had left Albany the preceding day at nine A. M. They were haggard-looking enough, both sleepy and hungry. No cars appeared, time wore on ; we chatted with the others, thought of chartering a stage-sleigh, and discussed whether it would be proper to travel on Sunday, when at last the locomotive appeared and announced that the track was clear. Soon after sundown we were off, and at eight o'clock were safely at home. And now I will tell you about a Sabbath in Hartford. My country eyes were much dazzled by the wondrously gay streets. Mr. Hastings announced a letter from Mr. Bushnell, which he read. It ran somewhat thus : That he had never complained of his lot as a laborious one, but never knew how pleasant was his work until he looked back upon it from that distance. Should he be condemned to perpetual idleness in the future, he should look back upon the past twelve years as the greenest spot of his life. He saw his own deficiencies ; he saw those of his church ; and trusted they might help each other to a better life. Thus far had he written on a Sunday evening in Paris, by his solitary fire, when two strangers from America came to announce Dr. Bull's death. " I was about to add, that your lives should be industrious, for they may be short, but

God has spoken, and you must listen to His voice." It was concluded in language of the deepest feeling, tender and earnest. Mr. Hastings's sermon, "Thy will be done on earth as it is in Heaven," made me think of many of the discussions I had with Miss P., and I wished she could have heard it. Mr. H. said, "A sister in the church returned thanks after an illness." This was supposed to be old lady Patton, who has been ill a few weeks, but no one seemed to have missed her from that front seat. Mr. H. did not allude to "Thine aged servant," but to "those this day restored to us, whose spirits have been with us," etc. I thanked him half sportively on Monday for remembering me in his thanksgiving, and he said he did mean it for myself and Buckland Bull. I do not believe he remembered the old lady at all. You see it is considered necessary to have public thanks returned for those who are safe from the heathenism of Vermont and Water Cure. I called at Mr. Wadsworth's this afternoon, and he made many inquiries about you. Mr. Cheney was there, and showed me a beautiful daguerreotype of his picture of Miss Wadsworth, but said it was not as good as the original. Mrs. Perkins came Monday to inquire whether water cure would help her sisters, who are both great invalids. Mrs. Stowe is very feeble, and has lost the use of her arms by a sort of paralysis. Miss Caty is as lame as ever, but these helpless ones intend starting early in March, and will probably go to Brattleboro' to consult Dr. W. We had a letter from Harriet yesterday. She was, as usual, in a great hurry, and preparing to go to Brookline to see some one in Linden Place, who was to have a tableaux party. The sleighing was fine, and they were to go in a great sleigh called the "Cleopatra." She would prefer coming home the middle of March, and talks of meeting us here with great pleasure. The visiting season is not over yet, although Lent commenced yesterday. It seemed to me like Vanity Fair, to wear a blue tarletan, with short sleeves and low neck. I must not run on any more. Much love to all my kind friends.

March 5, 1846.

Your most welcome journal-letter found me engaged in the worldly vanity of arraying myself in a thin pink dress with white roses, to attend a party at Mrs. Dr. Grant's. The blaze of chandeliers and the glitter of dress and mirrors almost blinded my country eyes, so long accustomed to the quiet simplicity of Stolz's three hanging lamps. Peace to his exit. May his light blaze more brightly in this dark and benighted world than ever his lamps did in Brattleboro'. Many kind inquiries were made after you. Dr. Hawes came to see Papa the other evening on business, and said that he was glad to hear such good news of Miss Catharine; he had thought she was destined for an early removal, but now that she had turned the corner, he felt persuaded that she would recover. Whether this was the corner at Mrs. Blake's, which is the only corner of much note in Brattleboro', or whether it was the first step towards recovery, the good doctor knows best. Mrs. Sigourney was at Mrs. Grant's, in her court presentation dress of light watered silk, trimmed in a manner perfectly unique, with lace and white ribbon. She was "glad to see you, dear, and most happy to know that your sister is improving." Mrs. Grant made a very pretty hostess in a dress of black velvet with a scarf of thread lace upon her shoulders, and pearls wound about her braid of dark hair. Mrs. Catlin appeared with her smiling face under a turban of white and scarlet. Miss Flora swung around in black velvet. Dr. and Mrs. Hawes were there, so there was no dancing, though many anxious glances were cast at the closed piano and the large room.

March 16, 1846.

I must snatch an hour from the care of Monday morning, to thank you for your welcome letter received Saturday. More especially do I thank you for the tidings that it bore, which sent me to church with a light heart, and I hope a grateful one. "I had been much exercised" (as Cromwell would say) upon the subject for several days, and I was more ashamed that my faith was so weak. "According to your faith be it unto you," and I do hope and trust that a few weeks more will find you restored to comfortable health. Every step of your course while under this treatment has been so kindly ordered that it would be ungrateful indeed not to trust for the remainder. Our river opened on Saturday, and in a few days we hope navigation will be resumed. The ice and water have gone off so favorably that even the most timid holders of bridge stock have had nothing to fear. I am sorry Dr. B. should have any practical illustrations of the word flirtation, especially from American ladies, who should knew better. My poor theory of friendship gets knocked on the head very often; if women will love admiration and attention better than self-respect, and men will be vain enough to love the least shadow of power better than rational conversation, then we must settle down on the old non-intercourse system. The water has been found in our well after eleven feet of blasting; it is now more than sixty feet deep. We have not used it yet, but the men think it will be pure, permanent, and abundant. I keep a general intelligence office for all water-cure information. I mean to charge the doctor roundly for my services, as it is the same sort of office that men and boys have who are attached to hotels and railroads. Write soon. Yours truly,

S. C. D.

November 6, 1846.

DEAR CATE, — We have been looking for a letter from you all this week, but I will not defer writing until yours comes, but rather endeavor to provoke you to love and good works. I have seen Miss Beecher twice, and she looks pretty well, but is working at a rate at which I know Dr. W. would shake his head. This afternoon she met about a dozen ladies at Dr. Hawes's, and detailed some of her plans,[1] and made

---

[1] Organization of the National Popular Education Society, of which our grandfather was President, and ex-Governor Slade of Vermont was General Agent.

some arrangements for a more public meeting to be held next week. I met Governor Slade at Mrs. Parsons', Wednesday evening. Father has returned from Boston this afternoon, and brought a line from Harriet, which I inclose. She writes very imploringly, as you see, and I shall make my arrangements to leave here a week from Monday. Mary is to buy me a hat in New York ; but I am at a standstill about an outer garment, whether it shall be a shawl or cloak. I have been on the point of buying a $60 shawl at Olmstead's, but hesitated ; and now I think I shall prefer a cloak. Our streets are lined with handsome shawls worn by *nobodies*, — a singular fact in the world of material philosophy, but well understood in the world of fashion. In all the storm of Wednesday, two gentlemen called to "see the ladies." They proved to be Mr. Flagg and Mr. Cheney. The latter is on his way to Boston, where he will remain at present. All unite in love. Remember me to my friends.

Yours,   S. C. D.

S. C. D. TO H. D. P.

March 30, 1847.

MY DEAR SISTER, — I have not much to record, for we have moved on very quietly since John left. Sunday was fair, though blustering, and we all of us made our way to the North Church, where in the morning we had a most peculiar sermon, and in the evening a very fine one upon Paul. Mr. Bushnell called Paul before his conversion a very Shylock of Orthodoxy, and touched off the great and good qualities of the man brilliantly. Yesterday afternoon I took Katy up to see Cousin Mary Collins, and her little folks. Katy was almost bewildered with the variety of playthings, and promised to repeat her visit with much willingness. I am happy to say, also, that she behaved with unusual propriety, and remembered the numerous injunctions she had received. This morning she is playing about the parlor, and goes often to an imaginary post-office in the corner, to send letters " to my mamma, 31 West Cedar Street." And how is the little cunning baby, who I suppose is now installed sole mistress of the nursery? Does she bear her honors meekly? or does the tiny hand wield the sceptre of power with the same inflexibility as the former one? Are her eyes still blue? Did not you enjoy "Dombey and Son," that dull, rainy morning? Cate sent it from New York, and we read it last evening with great delight. Poor Florence! Write us soon. As ever,

Yours,   S. C. D.

S. C. DAY TO MRS. H. D. PUTNAM.

May 12, 1848.

MY DEAR SISTER, — We are hoping to see you and the dear children soon. Father and Mother expect to go to Norwich on Monday, and will be absent all the week. You seem to have forgotten the postscript about Mr. Bushnell's sermon, or perhaps had not time to add it. I have a great desire to know how he succeeded, for it seemed one of the most important and difficult tasks he had undertaken. One of the papers speaks of it as brilliant and profound, or some such epithet. I suppose newspaper puffs would not be very discriminating; and I wait for abler criticism. Mr. Dana sent me this morning his speech on taking the chair on the opening of a Free-Soil meeting. Pray ask John, if he sees Mr. Dana, to thank him, and if my opinion could be of any value to him, I would add my earnest sympathy in this Free-Soil movement. I am likely to be enlightened on both sides of the question, for Mr. Smith sent me from Brattleboro', last week, his speech at a Taylor meeting there. Ellen has not returned, nor do we know when to look for her. Tom and Charles are still in Litchfield County somewhere. We shall hope to see you soon.   Yours very affectionately,

S. C. DAY.

M. F. DAY TO MRS. H. D. PUTNAM.

Sabbath Eve, October, 1848.

Dear Hatty, — We have been busy as bees, or your letter would have been answered before this. Sarah and Ellen are going to New York to-morrow if Ellen is well enough. They are going first to Aunt Penelope's, 52 East 15th Street, and if you go to New York in a week or two you will meet them. Ellen is somewhat better, and the change of air may do her good, perhaps as much good as medical treatment. Mr. Bushnell has given us two most beautiful and powerful sermons to-day on retribution of sin. "Though your sins be as scarlet, they shall be white as snow," was the text in the morning, and the sermon was occupied in combating the arguments of those who hold that the law of retribution is inevitable and immutable. The afternoon sermon was a beautiful exposition of the scriptural doctrine, Christ reconciling the world unto God by cleansing them from sin, and turning every one from his iniquities. It seems to me the sermons were two of the very best he ever preached. I am sorry you do not feel quite well. If you feel that you want me now and would prefer my coming now than later, just write and say so. This poor letter seems hardly worth the sending, but I'll inclose Lizzie's and make it worth something. Love to all. Affectionately,

Mary.

ELLEN DAY TO MRS. H. D. PUTNAM AND M. F. DAY.

Flatbush, February, 1849.

My very dear Sisters, — It is too bad, I know it is, that your kind letters should remain so long unanswered by me, but I assure you it is not because I have been forgetful of you, or indifferent to your letters. No, I have actually tried to keep you and all at home out of my mind as much as possible, for I have found my heart was not strong enough to bear the thoughts that would come. I did hope quite confidently to leave the 12th of this month, but feel satisfied it will be far better for me to take the doctor's advice, and remain until the first of March. I have felt much better this week, and happier, because my mind was made up to stay. To-night, just at sunset, as I was lying on the bed, aching from head to foot, a kind, delightful, eight-page letter was brought me from Emily Perkins, giving me such vivid pictures of all the girls and herself, and her employments. I was much interested in what you wrote in one of your letters about the Unitarian meetings, and also in hearing about the Californian expedition. I noticed in an extract from the "London Times" a notice of Mr. Kirk's sermon. If it is convenient for you to send me a paper, I should like one sometimes. Between you and Mr. Rockwood Hoar, I have heard a good deal about Mrs. Storer's party. I read the little paragraph about it to Mrs. Hoar, and the next day she read me her husband's letter. She is very kind to me, and we are great friends. She always expects me to come and sit in her room every day, and reads me parts from her husband's letters, and cheers me up when I need it. I liked her from the first, but it was not until Lydia was sick that I began to love her. Yesterday she read me a long letter from Miss Lizzie Hoar. Did you go to Mr. Emerson's lecture as you intended? I have been very much interested in reading a critique upon his writings in an old number of "Blackwood" that I came across. You say "we shall get home together." Do you say so still, when you hear I shall not return until March? Hatty pictures her pleasant parlor to me so delightfully that it almost makes me homesick. The handkerchief tied over her head was not the least unnatural thing. I trust the impending cold was driven off. I love to hear everything about the children. Dear little witches, how I should kiss them if I could get hold of them! Governor Seward was here yesterday, but very provokingly left just before dinner. Mrs. H. and I had had quite a frolic dressing, and hoping for something out of the usual routine. My love to Mr. Putnam. It was a pleasure to me to see his handwriting and get the little outside note. Love to Sarah Hubbard, Sarah Adams, and Martha Parker. What would I not give to hear her sing! Good-night, dear sisters.

     Yours affectionately,   ELLEN.

M. F. DAY TO MRS. H. D. PUTNAM.

April, 1849.

My dear Harriet, — I am so starved with cold I can hardly think, speak, or write, yet I must before twelve just tell you that I have safely arrived. I found Ellen suffering from rheumatism, or something like it. They all said they were glad to see me. Mr. Beecher spent the evening, and talked in a very entertaining manner. The Sunday sociable met at Uncle Terry's, and I enjoyed it more than I can tell. The subject was "The effect of suffering upon the character." We had a cloud of witnesses as to its effect on the Christian character, but the whole subject was not entered into. For our next meeting we are to study the historic parts of the Bible for illustrations of the power of suffering.

Later. — I have been interrupted for the last hour very pleasantly by a call from Mr. Bushnell. He asked after John and yourself with much interest. He says he means to possess his soul in patience while they hang him in Boston; and after he is dead he knows somebody will thank him. He is firm in that faith. Tuesday evenings Mr. Bushnell is to have a Bible class for all the young who wish to attend. I think I am young enough for that. Thomas has bought a slip at the North Church, and has chosen Livy and Sarah to sit with him, and says he has one of the most respectable families in the church. Mr. Bushnell wishes he could only have a wife and family of his own there, and talked up matrimony in the most earnest manner. Mother says I must not write more. My best love to the dear children and John.

     Yours affectionately,   MARY.

C. A. D. TO H. D. P.

May 2, 1849.

DEAR HARRIET, — As one of the four upon whom your burden of a letter was imposed this morning, I hasten to begin the sheet. We are very sorry to hear that Katy is languid; we should say it might be spring weather, if we had had any such thing, but to-day is certainly cold. If you can come on and bring Katy, I think perhaps Mamma will return with you to Boston. She threatens to go and stay until you are tired of her. I think it best, always best, to put her up to her resolutions while they are fresh, or they will soon die. The Legislature assembled this morning, and a Free-Soil Speaker has been chosen. We shall know before night, I hope, if our neighbor[1] is to be distinguished as his ancestors by the title of Governor. We are expecting the teachers[2] here this evening with a few other friends, but have made no other preparation for them than election cake, Mary's Naples biscuit, and lemonade. They leave here to-morrow morning. To-morrow is election day, — the day of parade, etc. Perhaps you know through the newspaper of Mr. Henry Ward Beecher's illness. A letter last night from Thomas Beecher spoke of him as better, but still very ill. Who could be taken from life just now that would be more deeply and widely mourned than he?

At this point another sister takes up the letter: —

Thursday morning. — Mrs. Sigourney's fair hand last held this pen! I wonder whether it will drop words of wisdom when guided by mine. Nobody asked me for *my* autograph, but the young ladies clustered round Mrs. Sigourney with the most admiring devotion, and listened to every word she uttered. One young lady, who said she had read of her as a "Hemans in poetry, a Hannah More in spirit," sat with

[1] Mr. Trumbull.
[2] The young women sent out under Governor Slade to Minnesota by the National Popular Education Society.

Mrs. S.'s little hand imprisoned in hers for half the evening, and her joy was complete when Mrs. S. gave her an order on her bookseller for "Dewdrops," or water drops, or some other sort of drops, one copy for each young lady. Mr. Bushnell was here enjoying the scene highly. Twenty Protestant Sisters of Charity, just on the eve of leaving for their missions of usefulness, was enough to excite any man; but Mr. Bushnell, who is so earnest and whose sympathies are so strongly in this movement, was unusually tender and feeling. We sung "While Thee I seek, protecting Power" most fervently, and then Mr. Bushnell offered prayer, commending all to the protecting Power, and beseeching for all present a self-denying, Christ-like spirit, and that those who were going forth to a life of self-denial might still rejoice in spirit, — as indeed they must, if filled with the spirit of Christ — and closed with a benediction that all hearts felt to be indeed a blessing. I heard Miss S. tell Mr. Bushnell that she was going where at least she should not hear any poor preaching. "No, indeed, for the Lord will preach to you in Minnesota," said he, tenderly. We all wished you could have been here. Miss F. shone the star of the evening in your dark merino. This morning we are trying to think of a suitable dress for Miss A. She had declined an appointment, but her talents are very superior, and we now find her wardrobe is very scanty. Ellen has given her her nice yellow straw, which she received with much emotion. I must go to breakfast. Love to all. Yours affectionately,

MARY.

M. F. DAY TO MRS. H. D. PUTNAM.

December 31, 1849.

Wish you a happy new year, you and yours, dear Hatty! ... You want to know all the gossip that it is not against my principles to relate. Last week when Mr. Beecher[1] thought of going away, the girls who had belonged to his Sunday evening class thought they would like to give him some good-by

---

[1] Rev. Thomas K. Beecher, who later married Livy Day.

gift. He had been teasing me for some time to make the girls in the " Now and Then " Society make him a dressing-gown, which he said he would have cut and basted at the tailor's, and we should only have plain sewing to do. It would be so gratifying to him, he said, to "put out one arm as he sat in lonely bachelordom and say, ' Livy made this sleeve, and Sarah made that, and Mary put this collar round the neck,'" etc., but I had given him no hope that we would ever humor him to that extent; but when he was going away I relented, and told the girls I would join them in sending him one as a gift. The girls met at Mrs. C.'s on Thursday, and made it, and wrote some capital hexameter verses to put in the pocket. If you had read a new poem called "The Bothie of Tober Na Vuolich," in imitation of which the verses are written, I should send a copy. The coat was sent to me for finishing touches, and I sent it to Mr. B. just at dinner time. Its arrival produced great excitement, Mrs. Perkins said. And after all he concluded to stay!! There are no parties here at present except small gatherings, sociables, and societies. We went to a very pleasant sociable at Mrs. Parsons's, Friday night. We have tolerable sleighing here now, and at eleven this morning we are going out to make some calls.

Affectionately,   MARY.

Catherine, the third sister, had become engaged to Rev. S. J. Andrews, and was to be married in April.

C. A. D. TO H. D. P.
February 4, 1850.

DEAR HATTY, — We were a little surprised to see Mother Saturday night, though we expected her enough to have oysters in readiness to cook when she came. Thomas very quietly laid down the silver on the table, and said nothing about it, and I very quietly went off to bed without looking at it. When I looked at the beautiful pattern this morning, I could hardly believe it was what I had looked at without expecting to get it. I am very much obliged and thankful to you and John for your beautiful present. If you do not sip some good cups of tea with them, it will be your own fault, because you don't choose to get them, or mine that I do not know how to make good tea. They will be a daily remembrance of you both. Are you not surprised to hear that Sarah Bell has fallen into the ranks of the engaged? Father accuses me of setting the ball going in this house, which has proved so fatal, but I think it is a Hartford epidemic, begun long ago.

Mr. Bushnell preached one of his *great* sermons yesterday morning, — "Their ears are dull of hearing, and their eyes they have closed that they cannot see." He is evidently more earnest and interested than usual. I do not know that he has anything unusual to encourage him, unless it be the warmth of his own heart. I am getting sleepy, and you must take an affectionate good-night for one and all.

Yours, KATE.

We have now reached a point in these Chronicles where the clouds gather heavily. Passing shadows have indeed fallen, — illness in the home and the griefs of household friends that closely touched their sympathetic hearts; but from 1813 to 1850 the immediate family circle had been unbroken save for the death, in 1826, of an infant a few months old. We know that such a grief is an abiding sorrow in a mother's heart, and would not speak lightly of it, yet one cannot read through the letters of these years and not be impressed with the happy serenity of the home. Now the youngest, the pet and joy of them all, was to be taken from their midst. Ellen had for a year or two been somewhat of a sufferer, and in the spring of this year, 1850, had gone again to New York to be under a physician's care. No one seems to have thought at first that her illness was of a serious nature. The sisters took turns in remaining with her.

NEW YORK, *March* 24, 1850.

MY DEAR MOTHER, — Your letter, with Kate's note, reached me Friday evening. You seem to be getting on famously with your preparations. I hope you will not get over-tired and sick. We shall come, if Ellen is well enough, in time for the wedding; but I begin to think that, hard as it would be for us, it will be best on many accounts that she should stay in New York until the middle of April. She may gain her strength very rapidly, and I hope she will; but she is now so weak that she cannot bear her weight an instant, and still suffers from constant neuralgia. The doctors say she is better, *decidedly* better, but she thinks they do not know. Her fever has gone and her pulse is good, but she feels very weak and has numb turns.

Monday morning, before breakfast. — I have only a few moments to say how Ellen has passed the night. She has been very restless and suffered in her head. Ellen sends love. Do write us soon. Love to Emily Perkins. I hope she is well by this time. Affectionately,

MARY.

Such letters could hardly fail to alarm those at home, and the oldest sister went to join the two in New York. We give her own words: "Letters from Mary awakened especial anxiety. Ellen had been suffering severely, but the cause was still a hidden one. The last of March, the evening mail brought a letter so alarming that it was hastily decided that I should take an evening train for New York. I reached the station just in time to take my seat in the cars. At New Haven took the steamboat, and reached New York in the early morning. It was a bright, beautiful Easter Sunday, and I met crowds coming from early service in the Romish churches as I went through the streets to the house. I found Ellen too ill for more than a short recognition. Pain had done its work, and she lay quietly reposing as if in sleep."

"Father and Mother were telegraphed for, but the service was imperfect then, and they did not reach New York until all suffering was past and the sweet spirit at peace."

We have not many letters written by this youngest sister, and what we have were mostly written during her school-days to sisters much older than herself. These letters are perhaps a little quaint and old-fashioned, but show a lovely, conscientious nature. We are indebted to two of her most intimate friends for sketches of her character.

Ellen, the youngest of the Day family, called so early from the turmoil of life, left a large number of relations and friends to mourn her loss. Her gentle ways, interesting mind, and kind heart were sadly missed among them. Because of the training and pruning of so many mature members of the same family, Ellen would have reminded one more of a hot-house plant than of a wild flower; yet her lively interest in whatever engaged her attention was evidently spontaneous. She was not given to half measures or apathetic manifestations. Her whole soul was thrown into her various pursuits. Her intimate associates were often amused, edified, and forced into sympathy by her zeal, which was outwardly displayed in kindling cheeks and emphatic tones. One of her chief charms was the readiness to perceive desirable qualities in her companions, and to find them a source of enjoyment. Her brief existence was a sheltered one, containing little room for rough contact with life. From her birth she breathed the atmosphere of benevolent enterprise, social culture, and intellectual aspiration. The influences of home, of school, of church, of companionship, were all in harmony. In the first principles of saving faith, she was taught by the greatest preacher of his time, whose intricate theology, happily, did not interfere with his unveiling of divine truth in its simplicity. To have found a more conspicuous example of systematic Christian nurture than that afforded by our dear, lost friend, would not have been an easy task.[1]

In a most delightful talk with another of Aunt Ellen's early friends,[2] we gathered much of interest concerning her, and also the family life of those days. A part of what was said is given as nearly as may be in this friend's own words.

Your grandfather had a most benignant face. I shall never forget the expression. I can see him as he sat in church; and I remember his prayers at family prayers. The tone of his voice was beautiful, — just a little tremulous. . . . That makes me think of something which surprised me more than anything which ever happened in my friendship with Ellen. She had a most angelic temper, and I never suspected that this was not natural. But once when I was staying there for a little while, she came into the room suddenly, and threw herself on the bed in a most terrible fit of crying. I tried to comfort her. She said "I did not think I should ever do so again." She said she had naturally a terribly quick temper, but she had thought she had overcome it. Ellen said she was with her sister doing something for her. Her sister spoke to her impatiently, and she threw the cup or bowl right down, and rushed out of the room. I know it was a great surprise to me, and it was a real comfort to me to know that she had these fits of temper sometimes. I think she was the most naturally religious person I have ever known in my life. Mary Hawes had her Sunday-School class come down to

[1] Mrs. J. Hammond Trumbull.   [2] Mrs. Edward Everett Hale.

their house, — that is, Dr. Hawes's house, — to a prayer-meeting. My mother was not given to such meetings, and I did not want to go, but I should not have dared to say that I would not go. But it was terrible business to me. All I could do was to compose a little address beforehand. Mary Hawes and Ellen made simple prayers, and told just what they thought of, and what they wanted. I do not remember anything so beautiful and natural. Mary Hawes and Ellen, who were both spiritually religious, were both brought up rather differently. Mary considered dancing as being wrong, and at our little parties she would sit with a sort of abstracted look, while the others were dancing. But Ellen was fond of dancing, and gay as anybody could be. There would not be but one or two large dancing parties in the course of the winter, but there were gatherings of people, of all ages, where we had charades. There was the "Now and Then," which was delightful. "Work and Play" was another of these clubs. The young people met to sew in the afternoon, and the gentlemen came in the evening. We used to call the large parties, "light silk parties." They did not cut their dresses low, but the girls would speak of a "light silk party" as being more gay than a common club. . . . You would not have called Ellen little, but she was shorter than I am. Her hair was light brown, a very soft lovely color. Her eyes were remarkable, quite large and gray, — a sort of greenish gray. When she was interested they changed their color. They must have had very large irises. When she wore blue it was remarkably becoming; that used to make her eyes beautiful. She was decidedly slight, and everything about her was graceful. That reminds me that she was exquisitely made in every way. It seems as if the framework must have been more beautifully put together than that of other people. . . . Ellen's hands and wrists were so prettily rounded ! I used to look at her wrists and think how round and soft everything was about her. . . . She was a particularly high-minded person. She lived really in the highest life. You could not conceive of anything like managing or planning. She must have had a great talent for friendship. I cared more for her than for anybody else. Perhaps living with such sisters had something to do with it. All of them were certainly remarkable women. Your Aunt Sarah! She was a most remarkable person when she was thirty years old. I remember she said when there was some company of young girls coming together, "I shall display a pair of venerable arms." At thirty years it seemed to me not an out-of-the-way expression, but in fact her arms were beautiful. Your mother was perfectly fascinating, with beautiful dark eyes. She looks more like herself now than most people do at her age. She was my Aunt Isabella's bridesmaid, and she was married when they were both nineteen. I was ten, and I shall never forget how beautiful I thought them both. . . . Something Ellen said showed how fond she was of your father. It was either when they were just married, or when the marriage was very near. "John is so perfectly lovely to all of us, and we all like him as much as he has made Hattie love him." We were reading some book, in which it was said that somebody kissed a lady's hand. I said something about nobody's doing that now, and Ellen said, "I am perfectly sure that John has kissed Hattie's pretty hand." . . . I have not said anything about the quantities of young people who used to be visiting at your grandfather's. I never saw anything exactly like that house. When the legislature met, there were always hosts of people there. The house seemed equal to anything. And they used to welcome everybody in such a pleasant, simple way. It will show you how simple all our life was in Hartford if I say that my allowance was a hundred and forty dollars a year only. From this I had to buy stamps and paper and everything. But I was entirely satisfied. I never felt shabby or ill-dressed. Just think of it! If a girl were going away from home, perhaps she would have more. But there was great simplicity in everything. I wish those times could come back.

During this spring, events followed each other rapidly. All arrangements had been made for Thomas to go abroad, and it was thought best that Catherine should be married before he left. It was a solemn wedding, and one of the sisters says "more like a prayer-meeting than a wedding." The carriage to take the brother to the station, to start on his foreign travels, stood at the door with the one to bear away the bride, and "tearful congratulations" were mingled with words of "sorrowful parting." A few weeks more and another daughter[1] leaves the dear old home to make a new one in Ohio; "and then the desolation of the home, the bitter mourning for those that were gone, will never be forgotten, nor can that time be recalled, even now at the distance of nearly half a century, without painful emotion."[2] Only the oldest daughter now remained with her parents, but the new homes were increasing in interest and joy, and the grandchildren began to make the Day house ring again with merriment.

In October, 1854, our grandfather had a slight stroke of paralysis. "He arose and dressed as usual, but could not speak; the family prayer of thanksgiving and confession and petition, raised daily for so many years, was hushed, but there was still the same calm and patient serenity in his face and manner." He rallied, but was much of an invalid through the winter, and on the first day of March, 1855, a second

---

[1] Mary, who married Heman Ely.   [2] Recollections, S. D. H.

attack brought his beautiful life to a close in this world.

In 1856 the last daughter was married to Mr. Alex. H. Holley of Lakeville. Now, the home would have been indeed a lonely one but that Catherine, with her husband and children, came back to live with her mother. Of these years, one of the grandchildren gives her recollections.

The house used to seem very large and stately to me. I remember when we lifted the heavy brass knocker to announce our arrival from the train : almost before it fell, the door would be opened by Grandmamma, who seemed as little as the house was big. She could not have been so very old, — under seventy surely, when I first recall her — but her false front, and the close-fitting widow's cap with long strings, always made her seem to me like the embodiment of old age. She had, however, a pretty figure, and quick, light step, and sharp, bright black eyes, which, though a good deal sunken, seemed as if nothing could escape them. We always went first into the breakfast-room, which was the usual sitting-room, for though there were two parlors and a library on the same floor, they were not often used except to receive calls. In the breakfast-room was the big, open "Franklin" stove with its shining brass tops and andirons, and under the window, by the side of it, stood the quaint old work-table, with its deep bag drawer, and smaller drawer above, with all its mysterious compartments. Perhaps the most interesting thing to me was the little silver bird, with a crimson cushion on his back, which screwed on to the edge of the table and held one end of Grandmamma's fine hemming in his bill. Then there was the big sideboard, with its curious narrow, deep drawers for wine bottles, and the central cupboard, into which I once crept to hide from my cousin Hattie. I was entirely hidden, I know, though the doors would not shut tight. The long garden back of the house was the scene of many good times for all the grandchildren, I fancy. There was the garden, and the lower garden, the latter filled mostly with fruit trees, and in the apple-trees I passed a great deal of my time. I was a great reader, and at home we had a very delightful library through which I roamed at will, and for that reason, perhaps, the absence of any light literature made a profound impression upon me. The library was filled with histories and all sorts of statistical reports, and the "office" upstairs was filled with law books. I used to search the shelves through and through for anything in the shape of a story, only to be disappointed, until one day I took down a shabby old book whose exterior and title had promised me nothing, and reading a few words, found myself soon absorbed in "Don Quixote." That book filled many lonely hours in my childhood's visits to the Prospect Street house. My dear grandmother thought all story books a great waste of time, and used to look at me sharply over her spectacles when she found me reading, to ask me if I could not "find something useful to do." There was a deep well on the stoop at the back of the house, which was a great delight to me. It was a long way down to the water, and as the stoop was roofed in and covered with vines, it was sometimes impossible to see the water at all. How I used to hang over the edge of this mysterious cavern, and weave all sorts of romantic tales of the happenings down there! I remember none of them now, except that I imagined an evil spirit lived there, and when it was so dark that I could not see any reflection, I would run quickly away for fear he would draw me in, but when I could catch sight of the water far, far down, and sometimes a little light, I would hang fascinated an hour at a time over the edge. There was always a bit of fear and awe encompassing me when staying in the house. A very different place it must have been when filled with the six daughters and son, all full of life and spirits. The latter part of Grandmamma's life she lived a part of the year alone with a companion, a Miss Delano, and life seemed very dreary to a girl of ten or twelve in that big house. There were long passages and corridors leading past empty rooms, and about twilight time, if called to go through them, I made short work of it, almost leaping through the passages, and then pausing outside the sitting-room door to regain my breath, and enter with an air of nonchalance. One very bright memory is of the Thanksgivings which we sometimes passed at Grandmamma's. The families were so much scattered that I do not think any but Aunt Kate's and our own were often there; but there were enough for a long table. I shudder now to think how much my Cousin Hattie and I ate. If thankfulness were measured by the quantity of food consumed, what grateful children we must have been!

In 1865, just ten years after the death of her husband, our grandmother laid down her cares, and a life that for some months had been one of pain and patient suffering.

An adequate description of her character seems impossible. She was the mainspring of the daily life of the household; yet in such unobtrusive fashion that few realized it. Her letters written to her daughters after they were married have not been quoted here, because she so completely put herself aside, and threw herself into their interests and small domestic details and difficulties, that they give us almost nothing of the life in the Day house which we have tried to picture. But they bear tribute to the dependence which all her children placed on her judgment, and the necessity they felt for her loving sympathy.

The old Day house seems a thing of the past, but the spirit of the home-life born in it, a spirit of loving, cheerful self-sacrifice, is living still in all its children's widely scattered homes.

APPENDIX AND GENEALOGICAL TABLES.

THE REV. JEREMIAH DAY OF NEW PRESTON.

HE following paragraphs are extracted from the "Connecticut Evangelical Magazine" for December, 1806, pp. 212-216: —

... "His father being one of the first settlers of Colchester, Jeremiah, when a boy, was employed in the fields during the spring, summer, and autumn, and in the winter went a distance of three miles to school. He early discovered a great attachment to books. At Commencement, after he had completed his fifteenth year, he entered Yale College and was graduated in 1756. After he left college he taught school in Sharon until the 1st of December, 1757, when he commenced studies in divinity with Rev. Joseph Bellamy, D. D., of Bethlehem. After a year and a half's study, some modest doubts as to his qualifications for a gospel minister led him to return to his former employment of instructing a school. In the spring of 1763, his only brother [Jonathan] died, and in his will bequeathed him a farm on Sharon Mountain. Having a taste for mathematics and natural philosophy, he here divided his time between books and hard labor. The aged farmers in that vicinity still speak of Mr. Day as useful to them in their profession, and yet, notwithstanding his improved mind, he cheerfully submitted to all the toil of the field. While in this situation he faithfully discharged the office of selectman. In October, 1766, he represented the town of Sharon in the General Assembly, and about the same time received a military commission. . . . Miss Sarah Mills, of Kent, the wife of his youth, to whom he had been married about three years, sickened and died in August, 1767. Not long before her death, he, with her, made a public profession of religion. Soon afterwards he renewed his attention to theological studies under the direction of the Rev. Mr. [Cotton Mather] Smith, of Sharon [father of the late John Cotton Smith, Governor of Connecticut], was licensed as a candidate by the Litchfield Association, and after preaching at several places, came to New Preston in September, 1769, and was ordained as pastor of that flock, January 31, 1770.

"In all his intercourse with his people he was grave, serious, and instructive. Wise as a serpent, and harmless as a dove, he was one of the most illustrious examples of ministerial prudence. As a divine he had a sound understanding, capable of deep research in the science of theology. Though not a fervent and animated orator, he was a solemn and impressive preacher. The serious could not hear him without attention, nor attend to him without improvement. With a clear, luminous method, he loved chiefly to dwell on the great doctrines of divine grace, and the distinguishing truths of the gospel."

JOHN COIT.

John Coit is believed to have come from Wales. He was in Salem, Mass., where he had a grant of land, in 1638. He removed in 1644 to Gloucester, but October 19, 1650, received a grant of land in New London, Conn. He died in 1659; his will was dated in August of that year. His children all seem to have been born in Great Britain before his coming to this country. His wife died January 2, 1676, aged eighty.

LIEUTENANT THOMAS TRACY.

Lieutenant Thomas Tracy was the son of Nathaniel Tracy, of Tewksbury, Gloucester County, England. Thomas Tracy was born in Tewksbury about 1610. He came to Salem, Mass., in 1636, went from there to Weathersfield, Conn., thence to Saybrook, and was one of the thirty-four men who founded the town of Norwich, Conn., in 1660.

THE HON. THOMAS DAY, LL. D., OF HARTFORD.

From the " Hartford Daily Courant," March 3, 1855 : —
" Thomas Day, the third son of Rev. Jeremiah Day, was born in New Preston Society, town of Washington, Conn., July 6, 1777. He was a descendant, in the sixth generation, from Robert Day, who came to America among the first settlers in Massachusetts, and joined the company of one hundred persons, who in 1636, under the lead of Rev. Thomas Hooker, first settled the town of Hartford, Conn. Thomas Day graduated at Yale, in 1797 ; read law with Judge Reeve at Litchfield, and afterwards with Judge Dewey, of the Supreme Court of Massachusetts, at Williamstown, where Mr. Day was tutor in Williams College. In September, 1799, Mr. Day came to Hartford ; read law with Theodore Dwight, Esq., was admitted to the bar in December, 1799, and immediately entered on the practice of law in Hartford, where he has ever since resided.

" In October, 1809, he was appointed Assistant Secretary of State (George Wyllys being the principal secretary) and in 1810 he was elected Secretary of State by the people, and so continued for twenty-five successive years, by annual reëlection, until May, 1835. In May, 1815, he was appointed Associate Judge of the County Court for the County of Hartford, and annually afterwards, except one year, until May, 1825, in which year he was made Chief Judge of that court, and was continued in that office by annual appointments until June, 1833.

" In 1818, as one of the senior aldermen of the city of Hartford, he became one of the Judges of the City Court, and continued such by successive annual elections until March, 1831.

" He was one of the committee who prepared the statutes of 1808, and by him the notes were compiled, the index made, and the introduction written. He was also one of the committee who prepared the statutes of 1821 and 1824. In

1805 he commenced regularly reporting the decisions of the Supreme Court of Errors; but he took note of cases in the latter half of the eighteenth century, and his reports cover a period ranging through more than half a century. At the June term, 1853, he declined a reappointment, and the Supreme Court of Errors were pleased to express their high respect for his eminent services and exalted character, and to thank him for his advancement of judicial science through his numerous reports and other legal productions, and for his uniform kindness and courtesy in all his intercourse with the bench and the bar. He edited several English law works, in all about forty volumes, in which he introduced notices of American decisions, and made other improvements.

"He was one of the commissioners to distribute the stock at the formation of the Phœnix Bank, and remained closely connected with that institution as stockholder and director to the day of his death. He was for many years one of the trustees of the Hartford Grammar School, of the Hartford Female Seminary, of the American Asylum for the Deaf and Dumb, and of the Retreat for the Insane. He was Director of the Connecticut Bible Society; President of the Hartford County Missionary Society, auxiliary to the A. B. C. F. M.; President of the Connecticut Branch of the American Education Society; President of the Goodrich Association, etc.

"He was an original member of the Connecticut Historical Society, and aided in its reorganization in 1825, being at that time its recording secretary. On the revival of the society in 1839, he became its president, and so continued until within a few months. He was a liberal contributor to the funds of the Wadsworth Atheneum, and its first president. The corporation of Yale College, in 1847, conferred on Judge Day the honorary degree of LL. D. It is not known that he ever made an enemy. He died at Hartford, 1st March, 1855."

APPENDIX

SOME OF THE DESCENDANTS OF ROBERT DAY OF HARTFORD.

Robert Day = (1) Mary ——. = (2) Editha Stebbins.

Thomas = Sarah Cooper.   Mary.   John.   Samuel.   John.   Sarah.   Mary.

Thomas $\overline{\underline{1685}}$ Elizabeth Merrick.   Sarah.   Mary Wells.   Sarah.   Ebenezer.   Jonathan.   Ebenezer.   Deborah.   Nathan.   Ebenezer.   Samuel.   Jonathan.   Abigail.

Elizabeth.   Thomas $\overline{\underline{1727}}$ (2) Mary Wells.   Abel.   Jeremiah $\overline{\underline{1772}}$ (3) Abigail Noble.   Israel.   Sarah.

Tamar.   Jonathan.   Thomas $\overline{\underline{1813}}$ Sarah Coit.   Noble.   Sarah.   Mills.

Jeremiah.
Sherman.
Martha.
Jeremiah.
Henry.
Elizabeth.
Mary.
Olivia.

Sarah Coit (Holley), b. Sept. 23, 1844.
Elizabeth (Seymour), b. Feb. 16, 1846.
Thomas Mills, b. Nov. 21, 1817.
Catherine Augusta (Andrews), b. Aug. 6, 1819.
Harriet (Putnam), b. Nov. 26, 1822.
Robert, b. Feb. 28, 1824, d. June 12, 1824.
Mary Frances (Ely), b. May 7, 1826.
Ellen, b. Sept. 7, 1829, d. April 2, 1850.

Daniel Jones.
Henry Noble.
Jeremiah.
Mills.
Thomas.
Charles.
Elizabeth.
Sarah.

APPENDIX

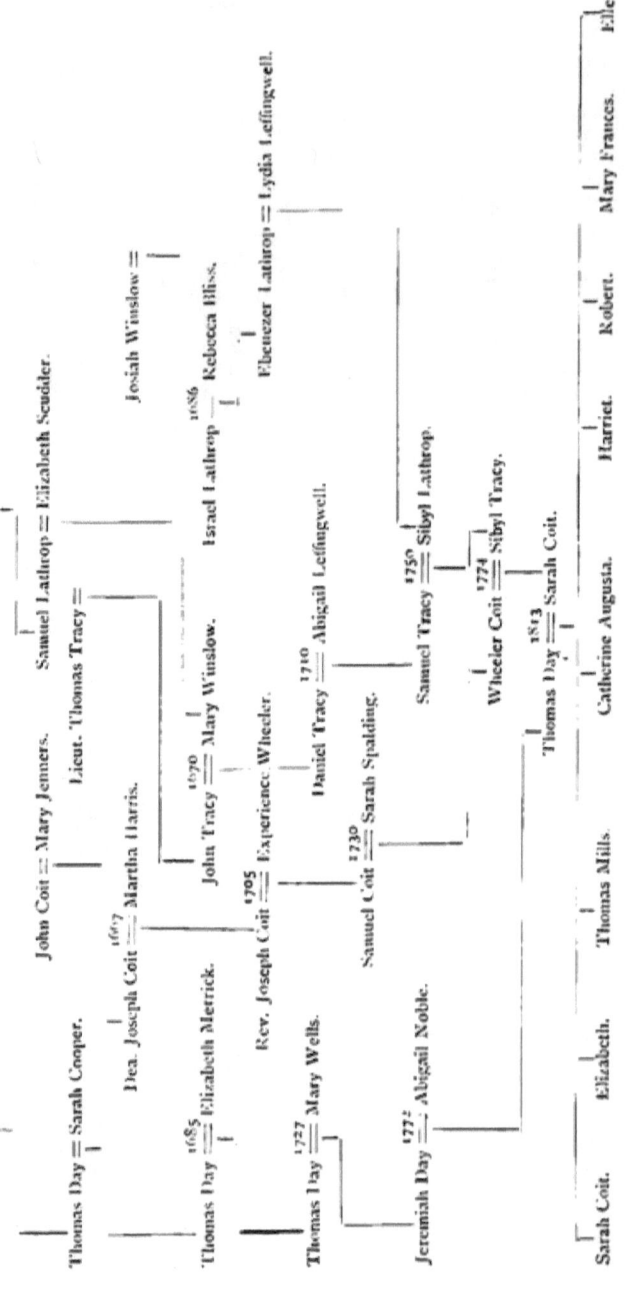

FAMILY TREE OF THOMAS DAY AND SARAH COIT.

www.ingramcontent.com/pod-product-compliance
Lightning Source LLC
Chambersburg PA
CBHW020307170426
43202CB00008B/526